In Old NEW ORLEANS

*Discover the exotic Crescent City
through her 19th-century arts and culture*

Edited by Kenneth W. Holditch

6.95

In Old NEW ORLEANS

W. Kenneth Holditch
Editor

University Press of Mississippi
Jackson

This book has been sponsored
by the University of Southern Mississippi

Library of Congress Cataloging in Publication Data

In Old New Orleans.

Main entry under title:
In old New Orleans.
(Southern quarterly series)
Bibliography: p.
Contents: New Orleans cemeteries / Peggy McDowell—
Minstrel dancing in New Orleans' nineteenth century
theatres / Kay DeMetz—George David Coulon / Judith
Hopkins Bonner—[etc.]
1. Arts, American—Louisiana—New Orleans—Addresses,
essays, lectures. 2. Arts, Modern—19th century—
Louisiana—New Orleans, Addresses, essays, lectures.
3. New Orleans (La.)—Popular culture—Addresses,
essays, lectures. I. Holditch, W. Kenneth. II. Series.
NX511.N39I5 1983 700'.9763'35 83-7025
ISBN 0-87805-186-4

Contents

Preface

In many ways, the nineteenth century *was* New Orleans' century, the era in which the culture of the city developed its distinctive character and matured to its peak condition. Earlier, the eighteenth century had given New Orleans birth and some growth but little progress under the alternate rule of the French and the Spanish. And afterwards, the twentieth century was to see the loss of many of the qualities that made the city unique not only in the South but in the nation as a whole, a loss of much of the individuality of the place, under the pressure and encouragement of some mayors, politicians, and numerous businessmen, all banded together in a selfish commitment to turning New Orleans into another Houston or Atlanta. But in between the century of its birth and the century of its decline, from 1800 to 1900, New Orleans developed economically, socially, culturally and artistically to become the Queen of the Mississippi. James Pitot in 1802 had written to officials in France his evaluation of the New World colony they had founded, then ceded to Spain, and would reacquire only to sell, almost at once, to the Americans: "Always uncivilized and listless in the past, the present begins to smile on Louisiana, and the future should make it a flourishing colony."[1] The next one hundred years were to make a prophet of Pitot, who very soon after writing his remarks was to become mayor of the city after the Americans had purchased Louisiana.

The following essays are intended to serve as an indication of some of the elements that contributed to making the Creole city with its ever expanding American population distinctive and great. The topics are by no means all inclusive—many important figures in major fields of achievement are missing. The intention is rather to give a sampling of various segments of the arts and culture of New Orleans when it was at its best. In some instances, the absence of the famous, whose lives and works have been thoroughly studied and analyzed in the past, is balanced by examinations of little known but significant contributors and fields which at last receive deserved recognition. The result, it is to be hoped, will exemplify the strange, exotic potpourri that has made the culture of New Orleans the object of abiding fascination for the rest of the nation.

W. K. H.

NOTE

[1]James Pitot, *Observations on the Colony of Louisiana from 1796 to 1802*, trans. Henry C. Pitot (Baton Rouge: Louisiana State Univ. Press, 1979), p. 5.

Art and Culture
in
Nineteenth Century New Orleans

All-Saints Day in New Orleans
From *Harper's Weekly*, 7 Nov. 1885, p. 729

New Orleans Cemeteries:
Architectural Styles and Influences

PEGGY MCDOWELL

Samuel Clemens as Mark Twain made the observation that "there is no architecture in New Orleans except in the cemeteries" in the 1883 publication *Life on the Mississippi*.[1] Mr. Clemens' witty evaluation of New Orleans' architecture is followed in the next chapter by this commentary:

> They bury their dead in vaults, above the ground. These vaults have a resemblance to houses—sometimes temples; are built of marble generally; are architecturally graceful and shapely; they face the walks and driveways of the cemetery; and when one moves through the midst of a thousand or so of them, and sees their white roofs and gables stretching into the distance on every hand, the phrase "city of the dead" has all at once a meaning to him. Many of the cemeteries are beautiful and are kept in perfect order.[2]

These were exceedingly kind words from Clemens, who, like a few other practical thinkers in the late nineteenth century, preferred the efficiency of cremation to the unhealthiness and expense of inhumation.[3] Clemens was well aware of the burden that contemporary burial customs had placed on the American mourner. He quotes a Chicago doctor to prove his point: "One and one-fourth times more money is expended annually in funerals in the United States than the government expends for public school purposes. . . . Funerals cost annually more money than the value of the combined gold and silver yield in the United States in the year 1880."[4] The vulnerability and pretentious pride of human nature reflected by funeral rituals were further illustrated by the sardonic wit of Clemens when, in his chapters on New Orleans, he concocts a story of an affluent undertaker and a recently widowed customer. Not to be

9

outdone by an acquaintance who had also buried a husband, the widow, through the wiley manipulation of the undertaker, spends far more than necessary for the sake of pride, prestige, and vainglory. This illiberal, albeit believable, assessment of burial practices in New Orleans is exaggerated; however, Clemens' tale aptly illustrates popular interests in funerary panoply in the late nineteenth century. Not confined to New Orleans, this interest in funeral rituals and related cemetery arts was widespread both in Europe and America. Like numerous ancient civilizations, nineteenth-century Western cultures will be remembered, perhaps, for their preoccupation with the commemorative arts—public, private, funerary and non-funerary memorials. Unless destroyed by pollution, vandalism, or urban blight, these monuments raised by our forbears to themselves, their loved ones, and their heroes provide us and future generations with an indication of their values and a museum of their arts. Attitudes since have changed, and the motivations that prompted the erection of such a large number of impressive commemorative monuments have been preempted by more life-oriented priorities. Samuel Clemens' elemental ideas about cremation were possibly an early prediction of changing attitudes about the then current funerary customs.

The early cemeteries in New Orleans were interesting to visitors to the city because of the large number of above ground tombs crowded within the confines of the local burial grounds. The styles of these tombs, monuments, and mausoleums provide the researcher with unique insights into the relationships between form, function, and artistic tastes. The reason most often given for the use of above ground vaults was the swampy condition of the soil. Architect and engineer Benjamin H. B. Latrobe made notes about the conditions in St. Louis Cemetery I in 1819: "There are two or three graves open and expecting their tenants; 8 or 9 inches below the surface they are filled with water and were not three feet deep. Thus, all persons here who are interred in the earth are buried in water."[5] Other nineteenth-century sources verify this condition.[6] There is no doubt that early burials in the water-logged soil of New Orleans were unesthetic and encouraged the use of alternative above-ground vaults. However, after proper drainage relieved much of the moisture, and new cemeteries on higher and dryer grounds were established, most New Orleaneans continued to build above-ground tombs. Inhumation became more feasible in the dryer soil and was practiced, but the majority of the funerary monuments erected in the second half of the nineteenth century were above-ground houses for the dead. Moist soil and watery graves, therefore, could not be the only reasons for the continuous use and popularity of these monuments.

One logical explanation for their popularity was the practicality of above-ground family vaults that could be re-opened and re-used for several generations of burials. After a proper length of time, a receptacle or back area within the tomb was used to contain the remains of former occupants whenever later burials within the same crypt were required. Cemetery plots with buried coffins do not as readily afford this practice. Land was valuable, and the families were often large and close. It was therefore economically and socially acceptable, even emotionally comforting, to use the same vaults over and over again. Whenever a family or an individual could not afford or did not own a family tomb, wall vaults and society or association tombs were available. Societies or associations were often formed for benevolent or social purposes; however, some were specifically organized to purchase and maintain large multi-crypt monuments in which the society members could be buried. Around the cemetery perimeters, wall vaults, which were sometimes called ovens because they resembled baker's ovens, were also alternatives to family or private tombs. This custom of using wall and society tombs was common in Spain and has been attributed to Spanish influences in early Louisiana.[7] Above ground crypts were frequently found in French and Spanish cemeteries, a condition which also made their use in Louisiana more acceptable to those of French or Spanish heritage.

Nineteenth-century attitudes about death in America and Europe were also responsible for the continuing emphasis on funerary paraphernalia. Theoretically, a tomb was an eternal dwelling place to shelter the fragile remains of family and self, and the nineteenth-century society was constantly reminded of the transitory nature of life and the inevitability of death. Across America popular sentimental ideas about death and the dead permeated prose and poetry. The poetry could, perhaps, be traced back to the influence of the Graveyard School; these maudlin poems, however, are far from being major contributions to literature. Publications such as *Frank Leslie's Illustrated Newspaper* and *Harper's New Monthly Magazine* routinely published poems like the following:

> The faces of the dead are fair,
> Though pale and fixed as sculptured stone,
> Their eyes have that appalling stare
> Which speaks of death, and death alone,
> In dreams, that half immortal state,
> In shadowy throngs they all appear,
> Who had my love, who had my hate,
> They once again are present here.[8]

Along with such melancholy poems written to and about the dead, popular publications printed images of weeping widows and children, graveyards, tombs and funerals. Several views of the New Orleans cemeteries can be found among these myriad illustrations.

In addition to articles, pictures, and poems in their daily reading material, Americans were also reminded of death by commemorative memorabilia displayed in the home. Memento mori included painted, embroidered, or printed death notices, hair immortelles, and photographs of the deceased draped in black. Mourning costumes and jewelry were usually worn by grieving family members for periods decreed by American or European customs. The result was a culture that was constantly confronted by death. These aspects of nineteenth-century America might be compared with ancestor veneration and funerary rites of passage in non-Western cultures. Cemeteries with their monuments reflecting tastes, styles, and status were another aspect of this phenomenon. Like New Orleans, numerous cities across America in the nineteenth century established regional metropolitan cemeteries set apart from churchyards. These cemeteries also accommodated large varieties of monuments, some for marking graves and some for above-ground burials. The New Orleans cemeteries by comparison have a unique character of their own, blending local, European, and American influences. By studying the earliest monuments along with those erected at the end of the century, one can see examples of styles, trends, and influences.

Although it was not the earliest, St. Louis Cemetery I, established 1789, is the oldest extant cemetery in New Orleans. At one time double its present size, St. Louis I now covers only a square city block on the fringe of the French Quarter. Close by, St. Louis Cemetery II was established in 1823 as an expansion of the earlier burial ground. As the city grew and new communities were settled and various religious groups desired their own cemeteries, new necropolises were started. Along with regional municipal cemeteries for specific sects, cemeteries were also begun by fraternal organizations, cemetery associations, and benevolent societies. Over thirty cemeteries were eventually established for the New Orleans population.[9]

Within these cities of the dead, a wide variety of architectural styles, sculptural, and ornamental arts are preserved. The above ground tombs range from modest, functional brick rectangles to granite mausoleums emulating temples and cathedrals. Students of architectural history can find a sampling of all the popular nineteenth-century revival styles and more. The influences that produced these varied architectural results are myriad. The choices of styles and types were primarily influenced by aesthetic and economic considerations. The earliest extant monuments in St. Louis Cemetery I are practical and modest. Most are local variations of fundamental types that can be traced to early European funerary designs. Their shapes were determined by their function: to enclose rectangular coffins. By far the simplest and most basic design, the rectangular box-shaped tomb with one or more vaults was often enhanced by pedimented facade, gabled roof, tiered stepped-top, or a barrel vaulted top. Podiums often elevated the tombs above the sometimes flooded grounds. Locally made brick was the most common and practical material for these early tombs, and brick masons were probably responsible for erecting and designing these simple monuments. Plaster and whitewash helped preserve and freshen the brick exterior. Wrought and, eventually, cast iron crosses, fences, and gates further enhanced these simple and charming monuments.

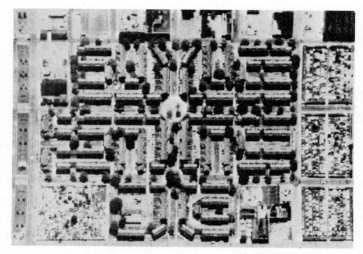

Aerial view of St. Louis Cemetery I and II
St. Louis Cemetery I is at lower left. Three blocks
of St. Louis Cemetery II are visible at the right.
Enlargement from Gulf Coast Aerial Photography print

View of St. Louis Cemetery I
Examples of early types of tombs
Photograph: Author

Although they continued to be reproduced in brick and stone throughout the nineteenth century, the modest tombs began to give way by the 1830s and the 1840s to more elegant and expensive monuments as family prestige, status, and fashion influenced funerary design. The revival styles became increasingly popular and inspired designers of funerary monuments in Europe and America in the early nineteenth century. The revival styles, especially the classical, Gothic, and Egyptian, having both aesthetic and symbolic appeal, were easily adapted to funerary design, and perhaps nowhere are the revival styles better represented than in the funerary arts. Each of the revival styles had its own period association or romantic connotation that could be broadly applied to funerary use—the purity and intellectuality of the classical, the spirituality of the Gothic, and the mysticism and stability of the Egyptian. Later in the century, styles inspired by exotic near-Eastern and Islamic design were also incorporated into funerary architecture. Of course, much of this interest in building monuments for individuals would not have existed without social and political reform and the rise of the middle class in Europe and in America. Individuals, regardless of their lineage, social status, religious views, or politics could have the kinds of substantial commemorative monuments previously reserved for the elite of the church and state. The rise of the individual and individuality was but one aspect of Romanticism. In art and architecture, the expressive use of the revival styles was another.

New Orleans cemeteries picturesquely reveal a blending of American and European traditions. Those citizens of French heritage, aware of the trends and styles in France, were especially influenced by the tomb designs in contemporary Parisian cemeteries such as Pére Lachaise, also known as the Cimetiere de l'Est, established in 1804. The majesty and elegance of this and other contemporary Parisian cemeteries exerted great influence on funerary traditions in France, England, and America. On a practical level, the realization of these elegant and artistic monuments was made possible by the availability of both materials and skills. Beginning in the 1830s, shipments of marble and granite from

Europe and other parts of America arrived more frequently. In the early nineteenth century, large granite quarries were opened in the eastern United States, and more quarries were developed in other regions as time and conditions permitted. Investors in these stone industries and marble contractors probably recognized the business potential of this port city. Although some marble workers were local men, others came to the city with the expanding stone industries. Newton Richards (1805–1874), an American trained builder, moved to the city in 1831 from Boston and New York. He established a marble and granite business and joined other "marbriers," French and American trained, who prospered in the city. Although data on Richards and other stone workers is limited, they left their names as builders on numerous tombs in the city as evidence of their skill. Thanks to men such as Richards, tombs in stone could be more easily and economically fabricated in New Orleans; citizens no longer needed to import ready-made monuments from other states or countries as they had in the past.

Jacques Nicholas Bussiere de Pouilly (1804–1875), a French trained architect, immigrated to Louisiana in 1833. A man of exceptional talents, De Pouilly was the first major architect to introduce the revival styles into local funerary design. De Pouilly's ideas inspired contemporary funerary architecture and reflected contemporary tastes. He is among the few well known New Orleans architects who were active on all levels of architectural design. From 1833 until his death in 1875, De Pouilly made his mark on the developing city. His contributions were recorded in part in a sketch book labeled "3 Nouvelle Orleans."[10] He found a sympathetic clientele in the Creole population but did not limit his talents to the French-speaking society nor to New Orleans alone. His varied and numerous designs include churches, private dwellings, and businesses. Ironically, of the many structures attributed to him, the best preserved testaments to his creative abilities are his tombs. The varied tastes of the New Orleans culture reflected in the tombs selected by his clients offered De Pouilly ample opportunity to display his talents. A large percentage of the designs in his sketch book are for tombs; some were built, others were destined to remain on paper.

De Pouilly used with equal facility designs based on the classical, Gothic, and Egyptian revivals. His designs grew out of his training in Paris, and it is probable that he studied briefly at either or both the Ecole des Beaux Arts and the Ecole Polytechnique. He also was exposed to the architecture in contemporary Parisian cemeteries, and he reportedly brought with him to Louisiana a book of illustrations of Pére Lachaise.[11] In nineteenth-century France, scholars and academicians promoted the study of period and area styles. Architectural students in Paris were exposed to a variety of designs and structures from many periods and areas of the world in reference volumes such as J. N. L. Durand's *Precis des lecons d'architecture donnees a l'Ecole Polytechnique,* and *Recueil et parallele des edifices de tout genre, ancien et modernes.* Eclectic romanticizing under an academic guise found its way into funerary design. De Pouilly's tombs have their origin in French traditions; thus the first impetus toward the revival styles in funerary art came from French rather than American sources. De Pouilly's tombs reflect and illustrate design elements popular in America as well as Europe and offer evidence that there existed international trends in funerary design—trends that reflected and embodied the widely spread and interpreted revival styles.

In St. Louis Cemetery II where the best examples of the earliest interpretations of the revival styles are located, De Pouilly's monuments stand out. Although examples of all the popular revival styles are illustrated, neoclassicism dominated De Pouilly's designs. He was probably encouraged in this direction by the majority of the local clientele, and he reveals his versatility in the use of classical prototypes. He drew inspiration from ancient Greek and Roman sarcophagi, columns, and temples. Of these the most impressive was the tomb that emulated a small temple. This type became popular in the 1840s because of the influence of De Pouilly. The neoclassical temple tomb that De Pouilly designed, as seen in St. Louis Cemetery II, is prostyle, that is, with porch on the front, and is elevated on a low podium with steps leading to a shallow portico. The pedimented roof is supported by two columns of a classical order. The vaults of one version are visible and are sheltered by the open porch. In other instances, as in similar French neoclassical

Left: Miltenberger Family Tomb
Right: Peniston-Duplantier Mausoleum
St. Louis Cemetery II
Designed by J. N. B. de Pouilly
Photograph: Betsy Swanson

mausoleums, a shallow "chapelle" precedes the vaults and bronze doors close the entrance. In France it was common to have an additional crypt beneath the mausoleum, a practice not feasible in New Orleans. Among De Pouilly's most notable neoclassical temple tomb designs in St. Louis Cemetery II are the Peniston-Duplantier (1842), Plauche (1845), Lacoste (1849), and Miltenberger (1850) family tombs.[12] Nearby are the Grailhe mausoleum (1850) revealing De Pouilly's interpretation of the Egyptian revival and the ornate J. M. Caballero mausoleum (1860) in the Gothic style. Numerous other monuments by De Pouilly are found in St. Louis Cemetery II and other local necropolises.

Grailhe Mausoleum
St. Louis Cemetery II
Designed by J. N. B. de Pouilly
Photograph: Ralph Hogan

Students who desire a broad overview of revival trends should start their studies with St. Louis Cemetery II and end with Metairie Cemetery. Metairie Cemetery, established late in the century, 1872, on the grounds of a converted race track, is the most elegant of the local campo santos. Its overall effect with lagoon, landscaping, and parklike setting is similar in character to other large American metropolitan burial grounds established in the nineteenth

century such as Greenwood Cemetery in Brooklyn, Woodlawn
Cemetery in Bronx, and Laurel Hill Cemetery in Philadelphia.
Although these other American cemeteries have a large percentage
of plots with underground burials, they, like Metairie Cemetery,

J. M. Caballero Mausoleum
St. Louis Cemetery II
Designed by J. N. B. de Pouilly
Photograph: Author

have numerous mausoleums of different sizes and styles surrounded by grassy lawns, shrubs, and trees. The parklike setting
and quiet beauty of the grounds appealed to city dwellers who
often visited the cemeteries on outings to sightsee and stroll among
the monuments. Greenwood Cemetery in Brooklyn even had a
twenty-five cent carriage tour for visitors and sold souvenir book-
lets and guide books. Proper behavior was expected, however, and
guests were usually informed about the rules before entering.

In New Orleans the crowded conditions of the earlier cemeteries, such as St. Louis I and II, are relieved in Metairie. Some of the
most sumptuous late nineteenth-century tombs are also found in
Metairie and comparable cemeteries in the eastern United States.
There seemed to be a final flowering of funerary arts between 1880
and 1920. The prestige-conscious generation of the wealthy who
grew to financial success after the Civil War pushed the funerary
arts to extremes of grandeur. These grand and somewhat ostenta-
tious mausoleums are frequently found in the prestigious cemeteries in the eastern United States. Similarly elegant structures,
visually enriched by varieties of granites and marbles, stained
glass, relief and free-standing sculpture and other ornate architectural details are also well represented in Metairie Cemetery. The
revival styles are present, expanded by the tastes of the late nineteenth-century clientele and the professional skills of firms that
specialized in designing, selling, and building tombs, mausoleums,
tombstones, and commemorative statuary. A tour around the oval
streets and pathways of this transformed race track provides the
viewer with a condensed history of architectural period styles lib-
erally reinterpreted and eclectically assembled. The Egyptian revival style is impressively represented by the Lucien Brunswig
mausoleum. Probably built in the last decade of the nineteenth
century, the Brunswig mausoleum is a granite pyramid opened by a
portal inspired by Egyptian design. On one side of the door
crouches an elegant marble sphinx, while on the opposite side
stands a marble vase and a female figure that points toward the
Brunswig name inscribed on the lintel. The Frank B. Williams
mausoleum created in the early 1920s was probably inspired by the
Egyptian pylon temples with traditional Egyptianized sculptural

Lucien Brunswig Mausoleum
Metairie Cemetery
Photograph: Author

reliefs and ornamentation. Greek and Roman temples abound and exhaust almost all the styles and variations of traditional floor plans; prostyle, amphiprostyle, and peripteral types are creatively interpreted as family mausoleums. Architectural orders include Doric, Ionic, Corinthian, Tuscan examples and eclectic combinations. A particularly faithful reconstruction of the amphiprostyle type (porches on the front and back) dates in the mid-twentieth century. The William G. Helis mausoleum is a reproduction of the Temple of Athena Nike from the Acropolis in Athens. The peripteral type with Ionian columns on all four sides is represented by the elegant

Chapman Hyams mausoleum built in the early twentieth century. Along with these and other neoclassical temples, monuments based on antique stele, exedra, sarcophagi, and columns are scattered throughout Metairie Cemetery.

Chapman Hyams Mausoleum
Metairie Cemetery
Photograph: Author

Medieval revival styles range from Romanesque-inspired mausoleums like the rusticated Joseph A. Walker mausoleum to the High Victorian Gothic style represented by the David C. McCann mausoleum. The most picturesque and romantic of the Gothic inspired designs is probably the Bentinck Egan monument that duplicates the ruins of a Gothic chapel. Mausoleum designs from near-Eastern

Joseph A. Walker Mausoleum
Metairie Cemetery
Photograph: Author.

David D. McCann Mausoleum.
Metairie Cemetery
Photograph: Warren Gravois

Egan Monument
Metairie Cemetery
Photograph: Author

Charles A. Larendon Tomb
Metairie Cemetery
Photograph: Author

or Islamic sources are also found among this montage of types and styles—see for example the Charles A. Larendon tomb and the Benton W. Cason mausoleum. These styles and others are unpredictably placed side by side, creating dramatic contrasts and enriching the visual effect. The revival styles have matured and have been finally exhausted.

With only a few exceptions, the great age of funerary architecture was over by 1930. After 1930 there was a decline in originality; stock designs duplicated in large numbers apparently served the needs of the typical client. Large public mausoleums became increasingly popular. Recent generations of Americans—highly practical in their concerns—have priorities and attitudes about death which are different from those of their predecessors. The last vestiges of romanticism in funerary architecture died with the last generations of the nineteenth century.

NOTES

[1]Mark Twain, *Life on the Mississippi* (New York: Heritage Press, 1944), p. 244. Looking back on his mid-nineteenth century riverboat experiences on the Mississippi, the mature Samuel Clemens first published his reminiscences of this period for the *Atlantic Monthly* in 1875 as "Old Times on the Mississippi." This version did not include any notes about the New Orleans cemeteries. A brief visit to the river cities from St. Louis to New Orleans in 1882 helped him renew impressions for the expanded version *Life on the Mississippi* published in 1883.

[2]Mark Twain, p. 247.

[3]Like many of his contemporaries, Clemens believed that illnesses were spread by bodies of the dead, and he supported this idea with quotes from several physicians. The idea that miasmas from cemeteries caused disease was widely believed in the nineteenth century. Ironically, the cemeteries might have contributed to the spread of yellow fever epidemics, not by the bodies of the dead, but by the mosquitoes that bred in the water filled urns and vases decorating tombs.

[4]Mark Twain, p. 249. Clemens had a penchant for quoting sources in this volume. It is difficult to prove whether these figures are true or whether the quote was accurate. The idea that Americans annually spent a great amount of money on funerals, however, was graphically presented. Clemens felt that cremation would help relieve the problem. As Mark Twain, Clemens expressed some rather shocking ideas which were deleted from the original 1883 edition. These are published as addendum in the 1944 printing, and in this appendix, labeled "The Suppressed Passages," Clemens wrote "You can burn a person for four or five dollars; and you can get soap enough out of his ashes to foot the bill," p. 412.

[5]B. H. B. Latrobe, *Impressions Respecting New Orleans*, ed. Samuel Wilson, Jr. (New York: Columbia Univ. Press, 1951), p. 84.

[6]For a concise review of this condition see Albert Fossier, *New Orleans: The Glamour Period, 1800–1840* (New Orleans: Pelican, 1957). A chapter of this book is

devoted to the "City of the Wet Graves," which is documented with numerous nineteenth century sources; see pp. 419–39.

[7]Leonard V. Huber verifies this in his chapter "New Orleans Cemeteries: A Brief History," from L. Huber, P. McDowell, and M. Christovich, *New Orleans Architecture, Volume III, The Cemeteries* (Gretna, La.: Pelican Press, 1974). Huber includes a photograph, p. 8, from a cemetery in Seville, Spain, which shows a society tomb and wall vaults much like those in New Orleans. (I also observed similar types on a visit to Spain.) Leonard Huber's pioneering research on the history of the early cemeteries is also found in a small booklet, *The St. Louis Cemeteries of New Orleans* (New Orleans, 1963), co-authored by Samuel Wilson, Jr.

[8]Ernest Trevor, "Dreams of the Dead," in *Frank Leslie's Illustrated Newspaper*, 16 Jan. 1864, p. 267.

[9]For a concise history of these cemeteries, see L. Huber et al., *New Orleans Architecture, Volume III, The Cemeteries*.

[10]This valuable sketchbook-scrapbook of De Pouilly's drawings and clippings is presently in The Historic New Orleans Collection. The sketches in this volume primarily date from 1834 through the 1860s. The book is marked by the number "3"; however, whether other sketchbooks existed can only be left to conjecture. The illustrations, which are primarily in ink, pencil, and water colors, are not always placed in chronological order. De Pouilly has been sadly neglected by researchers. An early study was undertaken by Edith E. Long and is published, in part, in a pamphlet, *Madame Olivier's Mansion* (New Orleans, 1965). Mrs. Long shared much of her data on De Pouilly with me, and I am grateful for her early guidance.

[11]This book, *Le Pere la Chaise ou Recueil de Dessins* (Paris, n. d.), is in the Leonard V. Huber collection.

[12]For a list of De Pouilly's monuments, mausoleums, and tombs, see page 73 of L. Huber et al., *New Orleans Architecture, Volume III, The Cemeteries*. This volume illustrates all of De Pouilly's major cemetery monuments.

Minstrel Dancing in New Orleans' Nineteenth Century Theaters

KAYE DEMETZ

When the Romantic movement swept America during the nineteenth century, it found intense expression in the Old South. Among other moods, this emotional revolution brought with it a proneness to sentimentalism, which was eagerly embraced by the plantation culture. The Romantic mind was a hedonistic one that brooked no visions of ugliness, and the dominant planter class was highly susceptible to such an attitude. In *The Mind of the South*, W.J. Cash comments on this fondness for fantasy: "Nowhere, indeed, did this Victorianism, with its false feeling, its excessive nicety, its will to the denial of the ugly, find more sympathetic acceptance than in the South."[1]

Southern aristocrats perceived their world, in its every aspect, aesthetically. A generation influenced by Sir Walter Scott equated its own agrarian society with the medieval manor system and its chivalric code. Architecture was inspired by the glory of ancient Greece and Rome. Duels of honor, the Confederacy, and Southern "belles" all were fashioned by the Romantic spirit, and, ultimately, even slavery was envisioned as attractive. As Cash further points out, perhaps even more important to the growth of sentimentalism "was the interaction of the Yankee's attack with the South's own qualms over slavery." The South had to "prettify the institution and its own reactions," had to "boast of its own Great Heart." Thus the Southern legend moved "toward splendor and magnificence, toward a sort of ecstatic, teary-eyed vision of the Old South as the Happy–Happy Land."[2]

Predictably, when the abolitionists launched their crusade against slavery in the nineteenth century, the South responded promptly with all the means at its disposal. Only a Romantic culture

could have pictured the life of the slave as idyllic as that in the
poetry of William John Grayson, in the books and articles of George
Fitzhugh, William Gilmore Simms, and James H. Hammond. Indeed, in overwhelming rebuttal to Harriet Beecher Stowe's *Uncle
Tom's Cabin,* no less than fourteen pro-slavery novels were subsequently published.

In particular, the magic of the theater was an ideal medium of
expression for the South's refutations of anti-slavery, and one of the
most enduring idealized versions of slavery found its way to the
stage almost immediately in the form of the minstrel show. The
happy black man singing, dancing, playing music, and telling jokes
provided the perfect retort for any Yankee accusations against slavery. This romanticized concept of the southern slave is epitomized
in a remark of Southern apologist George Fitzhugh: "Slaves too
have a valuable property in their masters. . . . He is bound to support them, to supply all their wants, and relieve them of all care for
the present or future."[3] The carefree minstrel man, then, was the
embodiment of a widespread attitude in the South that slavery was
a pleasurable state for the black race.

Although it is difficult to verify, there is a widely accepted belief
that minstrelsy originated some time between 1828 and 1831 when
Thomas Dartmouth Rice, a white actor, imitated onstage the song
and dance of a young stable slave. According to Carl Wittke, because Rice "gave the first entertainment in which a black-faced
performer was not only the main actor, but the entire act," the title
of "father of minstrelsy" has been bestowed upon him.[4] Later performers elaborated upon this style of characterization until the
full-fledged minstrel show was born during the 1840s.

Certainly a dancing slave is a happy slave, and from the beginning the dance element was emphasized in minstrel routines. In
fact, Marshall and Jean Stearns, commenting on that initial minstrel
character called "Jim Crow," remark that "A few hearings of the
tune . . . made it reasonably clear that the dance, not the melody,
made Jump Jim Crow a national craze."[5] There is enough reference
in the "extravaganza's" song to the method of executing the dance
steps to indicate that the dance itself was possibly the strength of

the routine. The words and extant illustrations of Rice suggest some very lively dancing with particular emphasis on the legs and feet in this characterization.

> Now fall upon yo' knees/Jump up an' bow low. . . .
> Put yo' han's upon yo' hips/Bow low to yo' beau. . . .

And the chorus describes rather animated and jubilant steps.

> Wheel about, turn about/Do jis so,
> An' every time I wheel about, I jump Jim Crow![6]

Hans Nathan's description of Jim Crow's dancing also connotes a performer with a convivial personality.

> Rice, according to his own words, wheeled, turned, and jumped. In windmill fashion, he rolled his body lazily from one side to the other, throwing his weight alternately on the heel of one foot and on the toes of the other. Gradually, he must have turned away from his audience, and, on the words "jis so," jumped high up and back into his initial position. While doing all this, he rolled his left hand in a half-seductive, half-waggishly admonishing manner.[7]

As minstrel acts developed and gained popularity, the dance element appears to have retained its usefulness as a prime ingredient within the routine. Extant scripts of the skits contain at least one or two dances, and playbills and newspaper ads rarely fail to mention the dancing.

Carl Wittke points out in *Tambo and Bones* that by mid-nineteenth century minstrelsy was "monopolizing the attention of the great majority of American theatre-goers." He comments further that this form of entertainment "always enjoyed its greatest vogue in the South."[8] Certainly nowhere in the South was the minstrel show more popular than in New Orleans, Louisiana, the center for the Southern "theatrical circuit." Though it was a growing urban community, its culture was firmly rooted in the plantation tradition. With nineteen English language theaters operating during the pre-Civil War "Golden Age,"[9] New Orleans certainly qualified as a major theater city. For over half a century audiences watched this sentimentalized version of slavery develop from a simple one-man song and dance act to a full evening of elaborately staged minstrel shows involving up to one hundred performers.

Although the dancing minstrel man was not a sufficient answer for the abolitionists, this cheerful stage personality did ultimately serve several important functions in the annals of the American theatre. As one of America's first indigenous theatrical forms, minstrelsy helped to lay the foundation for vaudeville and burlesque. The peculiar style of minstrel dancing played a major part in the evolution of tap dancing. It provided black performers an entrance into a business generally restricted to the white race. And, finally, the minstrel routines yielded a large body of folk music and dance to this country and to the theatrical world in general. Minstrel dancing, then, represents a significant contribution to the American theater.

The engagements of selected minstrel performances in New Orleans offer examples of the increasing importance of the dance aspect of these presentations in the South. The purpose here is to examine some typical productions during the pre-Civil War period in the hope of affording some insight into the use of dance within the minstrel form. As abolitionists protested, these dancers paraded merrily across New Orleans' English language stages in growing numbers and for longer portions of the evenings' entertainments—defying the notion that slavery was anything but a happy state. Even a brief probe into the history of these performances suggests that the Romantic spirit was, indeed, alive in this vital southern theater center.

Abolitionist periodicals had barely begun attacking slavery when the first minstrel dancer appeared on New Orleans theater bills. These initial dances were usually solo routines performed as entr'acte pieces, that is, between the various acts on the evening's bill. Later, the song and dance presentations expanded into "production numbers" executed by large groups of dancers as part of the complete minstrel show. William Lloyd Garrison began preaching his crusade for freedom in the *Liberator* in 1834, and, interestingly enough, by April of the following year "Daddy" Rice was offering his minstrel "extravaganza" *Jim Crow* on New Orleans stages. His act was apparently popular because the New Orleans *Bee* records that he even performed it in French in 1835: ". . . at the desire of several French families, and in compliance with their wishes, Mr. Rice will, for the first time, sing his extravaganza of *Jim Crow,* in French and English."[10] By this time he had become well known for the way he "jumped Jim Crow," and the character was performed repeatedly during his visits to the English language theaters in 1835, 1836, 1838, and 1842.

As they achieved more widespread success, brief extravaganzas like *Jim Crow* were extended into more complex dramatic pieces somewhat resembling farces. Such minstrel compositions were referred to as "Ethiopian operas," "black operas," "comic operas," and "Ethiopian dramas." Two of these works produced in New Orleans were written and popularized by Daddy Rice. Both scripts invariably call for several characters to sing and dance.

The plot of *Oh! Hush!* undoubtedly exists for the songs, dances, and characterizations. The piece introduces the minstrel character of Gumbo Cuff, which Rice played during his New Orleans visits. The dandy Sambo Johnson pays a visit to Miss Dinah Rose, unaware that Mr. Cuff has been there earlier courting her. To avoid a confrontation, Rose hides Cuff in a closet, but jealousy gets the better of him and a fight ensues between the two suitors. By the end of the single act, however, the argument is settled and Cuff suggests a dance.

> Cuff: . . . But dar's no use to keep up grievances, since love am all by chance. So jest hand down de fiddle, Pete, and let us had a dance. . . . (They form and go through a reel.)[11]

Here the brief drama ends abruptly when Cuff breaks a fiddle over Johnson's head.

Bone Squash (sometimes called *Bone Squash Diavolo*) is a somewhat longer musical piece containing considerably more dancing, but a plot that is no less nonsensical. The protagonist, Bone Squash, sells his soul to the devil and with his newly acquired wealth decides that he is ready to take on a wife. Two obstacles present themselves in the course of the play: his loved one's boyfriend and his creditor the devil. As with *Oh! Hush!* the importance of the plot is secondary to that of the songs, dances, and characterizations. Except for the wedding dance, the motivations for the dances are tenuous at best. The first number takes place soon after the opening scene when Jim Brown brags about his singing talent. After the first chorus, "All dance the shuffle." The second verse and chorus are sung and, again, "all dance and exit. . . ."[12]

In Scene Three, Bone has invited his friends to celebrate his betrothal to the reluctant Junietta. In the course of the revelry they all join in a song and dance.

> Enter Jim Brown with his fiddle. . . .
> During the symphony, they all dance. . . .

The lyrics of the song designate the dancing that follows.

> Come, saw upon de fiddle now,/Old Jim Brown.
> Till we cut de pigeon wing,/and hab a break down.
> . . . .
>
> Bone Squash take de lead,/And we all will begin.
> DANCE.
> . . . .
>
> While we dance at de wedding,/Ob ole Bone Squash.
> (Dance, as before.)[13]

Here the script even indicates the various formations and positions of the participating characters. At this point, both Spruce Pink, Junietta's boyfriend, and the devil appear and the obvious conflicts result. Ultimately, in deus ex machina finish, Bone Squash ascends with the devil in a balloon and pitches him out on the way up.

Rice included *Oh! Hush!* in his repertoire during his 1835 and 1836 visits to New Orleans. Nearly all these presentations announced by the *Bee* listed Rice in the role of Gumbo Cuff. Similarly, the *Bee* notes that Rice played the role of Bone Squash.[14]

A lad named John Diamond was one of the best known solo minstrel dancers of the early 1840s. According to Hans Nathan, Master Diamond "prided himself on his skill at negro dancing," though his popularity probably resulted as much from his participation in dance competitions as from his proficiency as a dancer. When he made his New Orleans debut in 1841 at the St. Charles Theatre, "Master" Diamond initially was billed insignificantly as an entr'acte routine. On the evening of his opening, however, the theater management focused on his dance act by announcing in the *Picayune* a dance contest: "Master Diamond hereby challenges any person in America to a trial of skill at negro dancing, in all its varieties, for the sum of $200 to $1000."[15] His dance act received more attention when the challenge was answered nine days later. "Master Diamond's challenge having been accepted A Grand Match Dance! ! For a wager of Five Hundred Dollars will come off between Master Diamond and Mr. Mercer of Kentucky; in which will be introduced every variety of double-shuffle, heel-and-toe— 'Ole Virginny Breakdowns.' "[16]

In his memoirs the famous theater manager Solomon Smith notes how lucrative this double dance act turned out to be: ". . . under the auspices of Barnum, they got up a humbug dancing-match for a pretended wager of $500 a side, and introduced a supernumerary, with his face blacked, to dance with and be beaten by that jewel of dancers, which produced a return (I should think) of nearly $2000!"[17] From the *Picayune* one might receive the impression that, at this point, minstrel dancing was obscuring other acts on the bill.

> If a sterling play and farce will draw $300 to the St. Charles, and a negro dancer will draw $1500, which bill is the manager likely to offer? . . . How came Jim Crow to make a fortune? . . . Which received most applause the other night, Bulwer's play, Bellini's music, or the negro dance? Legitimate critics can of course tell us all about how these things should be arranged.[18]

In the next day's issue the *Picayune* was still exultant over the public's esteem for dance by black-faced performers.

> Let those who cry out against the degradation of the St. Charles stage by negro dancing, show now some positive evidence that they have legitimate taste, and go to see Ranger. One of the most, if not *the* most exquisitely finished comedians of the day, is now "scattering pearl" in New Orleans, and "the Temple" is empty!—for who would scramble for pearls while they are outshone by the superior lustre of a *Diamond!*[19]

The account of another New Orleans theater manager, Noah Ludlow, indicates that Diamond had won some favor with audiences.

> "Master Dimond," [sic] . . . with blackened face and hands, performed

negro dances, to the no small delight of many who admired such exhibi-
tions of suppleness. He could twist his feet and legs, while dancing, into
more fantastic forms than I ever witnessed before or since in any human
being.[20]

Despite the fact that the dancing match was exposed as a ruse,
Diamond was apparently successful enough to obtain an April engagement at the American Theater and a return visit for the following winter at both English language houses. Perhaps Diamond and
the managers had begun to realize the drawing power of such
"dance duels," for the dancer returned in December of 1841 with a
partner to rival his dancing. From December through early January
the "two celebrated Professors of Niggerology" staged competition
routines.

Even though their dancing, as an entr'acte, shared the bill with
other acts, theater ads consistently drew attention to their presentations. For example, the 1 January 1842, *Commercial Bulletin* announced the "great contention" dance between Diamond and San-
ford. For their final appearance the team was listed as only one of
four acts, but the 4 January *Commercial Bulletin* heralded the
minstrel number as a "Grand Match Dance, Or Trial of Skill in
every variety of Double Shuffle, Heel and Toe Genus and Ole
Wirginny Break downs, between Master Diamond and Mr. San-
ford. . . ."

By the following year these individual minstrel acts inevitably
had evolved into a quartette, and the first minstrel company became a featured item on the bill. The group that is generally con-
ceded as the "original" company appeared in New Orleans in 1843,
the same year of their initial appearance in New York. The Virginia
Minstrels played at the St. Charles in December, sharing the bill
with other presentations during the evening. Dance was advertised
as one of the company's attractions: "Virginia Minstrels 'With their
unique Accompaniments and DANCES.' "[21] One playbill announced more specific details on the dancing: "with a Great Trial
Dance, Between Messrs Durand, Christy, Pearce and Daniel."[22]

Minstrel entertainments achieved prominence in New Orleans
during the 1850s. This popularity continued during the early sixties
even after the outbreak of the Civil War. The nation responded

with passion to the publication of Harriet Beecher Stowe's *Uncle Tom's Cabin*, and remonstrance from pro-slavery groups was intense. As might be expected, several dance routines were uniformly included in the repertoire of all minstrel companies. Kunkel's Nightengale Opera Troupe, which visited the City early in the 1850s, provides an example. The 17 January 1853, *Commercial Bulletin* specifically notes the dance offered by the minstrel group when they played at the American Theater: "In addition to the Vocal Music DANCING of a very high order, displaying Grace, Agility and Elegance, in lieu of mere physical strength or endurance, will be propounded." When the Campbell Minstrels appeared in New Orleans during November of 1855, local newspapers mentioned dance in reviews and advertisements almost daily. For example, a review in the 13 November *Picayune* made special mention of two of the company's dance presentations: "Mr. Cotton, convulsed the audience with the comicality of his *Bob Ridley* song and dance. The grand 'Railroad' gallopade [a type of dance] was 'some;' but this cannot be described—to be appreciated, it must be seen and heard." The following day the *Picayune* referred to "the dancing of Tom Peele and Matt," who were featured minstrel dancers. By Thursday's edition the *Picayune* was describing the dancing as one of the "leading features of this as of the former bills."[23]

In addition to general references to the dancing, a particular dance routine often received special attention. The 15 November 1855 *Picayune* review closed with the reminder: "Everybody should see Cotton in 'Bob Ridley.' " And on 18 November the *Picayune* called attention to still other dance presentations on the minstrel bill: "His [Mr. Peel's] dancing, *a la Soto*, Elssler and Ciocca, in the Cachuca, the Bolero, the pas Ecossaise, &c, is inimitable in its way. . . ."

During the late 1850s minstrel troupes were booked so frequently at New Orleans theaters that often rival companies played concurrently in the City. At this point in their development minstrel presentations made up a full evening's entertainments. In 1857 two nationally known companies visited: Matt Peel's Campbell Minstrels returned and competed with Rumsey and New-

comb's Campbell Minstrels. Both groups included dance in their
respective programs.

During the Matt Peel engagement at Spalding and Roger's
Amphitheater, newspaper accounts reveal that audiences witnessed a considerable amount of dancing. "Burlesque dances . . . a
Virginia Break down . . . Darkies Festival Dance . . ." and more of
the "Essence of Old Virginia" all were advertised in the 6 October
1857 *Picayune*. Several in the company apparently possessed dance
skills, because the *Picayune* records that a variety of performers
executed a number of different dances. The 27 October 1857 edition reports that "Master T. J. Peel will dance a Virginia Reel, in his
own inimitable manner. . . ." Three weeks later the paper records
that "Tom [probably Peel] will dance his burlesque Cachucha . . ."
and "Sexton will Dance his 'Essence of Virginia'. . . ."[24] Another
dance was added for the 18 November show. Ned Orrin and a
Master George executed a "Scotch Pas de Deux."[25]

Rumsey and Newcomb's group, performing in New Orleans at
the same time, offered a show divided into three parts: one segment
was completely devoted to dance and another partially to dance.
The evening's second portion was titled "Terpsichorean Divertise-
ments" and consisted of Rumsey, Newcomb, and Ritter in various
dances. Part III featured at least two major dance pieces: the
"Essence of Old Virginny," a breakdown composed by William W.
Newcomb himself and a rendition by a Richard Carroll, who was
advertised as the "Burlesque, Fancy, and greatest Jig Dancer now
living. . . ."[26]

Certainly George Christy's group should be listed among the
best remembered of all minstrel companies. The troupe was playing at the New Orleans Academy of Music when the Civil War
broke out in 1861. The format of their program hints that an evening
at the theater was now the reverse of the situation prevailing when
the early minstrel performers presented song and dance routines
between longer dramatic pieces. For example, during their engagement in New Orleans the Christy Minstrels advertised several
"Terpsichorean Representations," but only one farce. The dancing
included a "Secession Polka" by George Christy and Master Leon,
a "Pas de Fascination" by Master Leon, the "Essence of Old Vir-

ginny" by W. Arlington, and a finale by the complete company
entitled the "Plantation Song and Dance to the music of 'Dixie's
Land.' " Along with the other standard minstrel acts of songs and
instrumental renditions, the farce *The Black Statue* was the sole
dramatic offering on the bill.[27]

One of the last minstrel companies to appear in New Orleans
during the theatre's pre-War "golden era" was Duprez and Green's
New Orleans and Metropolitan Minstrels and Brass Band Com-
bined. Though only one item was listed as being specifically a
dance sequence, the fact that it was entitled the "New Medley
Dance" suggests that it comprised a number of dances.[28] This piece
may have been too meagre an offering for audiences, because additional dancing was added later. The 16 January 1863 *Daily True
Delta* announced that "COMMODORE FOOTE AND COL.
SMALL . . . will appear in connection with the world-renowned
DUPREZ & GREEN'S . . . MINSTRELS, and continue EVERY
NIGHT until further notice. . . ." Although the presentations apparently were not in the minstrel style, the Foote and Small act did
provide additional dancing with their "Scotch Dance" and "Double Irish Jig."

Evidently the popularity of minstrel shows remained high in
New Orleans. Before concluding their engagement there Messrs.
Duprez and Green announced plans to establish their troupe permanently in the City that very next season. During the Civil War,
however, managers and troupes began to retreat to the North and
many of the theaters began to close. As theatrical activity returned
to post-war New Orleans, minstrel shows bore less and less resem-
blance to the productions mounted earlier in the century. The
emphasis in these new, large-scale productions was more on spec-
tacle and less on the actual character of the Negro. Arguments of the
past, as Wittke observed, had little place in the New South.[29]

Perhaps the minstrel man was not a perfect reflection of nature,
but his image offered some veracity. His dances, though originally
performed by white actors, were born of the ante-bellum slave
society.[30] They were, indeed, the black individual's dance steps
executed in a manner that the Romantic Southerner envisioned as
the quintessence of the slave personality.

When Henry W. Bellows spoke to the American Drama Fund Society in 1857 of "the moral necessity of being happy," he suggested the theater as a means of "removing us from the region of the actual to that of the ideal." Thus, when abolitionists accused, the minstrel man—"omitting what is commonplace, irrelevant, or simply painful"—danced.[31] And, while he danced, he offered New Orleans—and the Old South—one last look at a world that only the Romantic mind could have appreciated.

NOTES

[1] W. J. Cash, *The Mind of the South* (New York: Knopf, 1941), p. 82.

[2] Cash, pp. 82–83, 127.

[3] *Sociology for the South, or the Failure of Free Society* (Richmond, Va.: A. Morris, [c. 1854]), as quoted in Edmund Wilson, *Patriotic Gore: Studies in the Literature of the American Civil War* (New York: Oxford Univ. Press, 1962), pp. 348–49.

[4] Carl Wittke, *Tambo and Bones* (Westport, Conn.: Greenwood Press, 1930), p. 20.

[5] Marshall and Jean Stearns, *Jazz Dance* (New York: Macmillan, 1968), p. 42.

[6] Stearns, pp. 40–41.

[7] Hans Nathan, *Dan Emmett and the Rise of Early Negro Minstrelsy* (Norman: Univ. of Oklahoma Press, 1962), p. 52.

[8] Wittke, p. 60, 82.

[9] At that time, New Orleans was divided into two sectors: English and French. This study examines only those theatrical activities in the English-speaking zone.

[10] New Orleans *Bee*, 11 May 1835.

[11] Thomas D. Rice, *Oh, Hush! Or, The Virginny Cupids*, ed. Charles White, English and American Drama of the Nineteenth Century (New York: Happy Hours Co., [1873?]), iii.

[12] Thomas D. Rice, *Bone Squash*, arranged by C. White, English and American Drama of the Nineteenth Century, 1 (New York: Samuel French, [1881?]), i.

[13] Rice, *Bone Squash*, I, iii.

[14] New Orleans *Bee*, 1 Mar. 1836.

[15] New Orleans *Picayune*, 10 Jan. 1841.

[16] New Orleans *Picayune*, 19 Jan. 1841.

[17] Solomon Smith, *Theatrical Management in the West and South for Thirty Years* (1868; rpt. New York: Benjamin Blom, 1968), p. 155.

[18] New Orleans *Picayune*, 22 Jan. 1841.

[19] *Picayune*, 23 Jan. 1841.

[20] Noah Ludlow, *Dramatic Life as I Found It* (1880; New York: Benjamin Blom, 1966) p. 533.

[21] St. Charles Playbill, 21 Dec. 1843, Harvard Theatre Collection.

[22] St. Charles Playbill, 17 Dec. 1843, Harvard Theatre Collection.

[23] *Daily Picayune*, 15 Nov. 1855.

[24] *Daily Picayune*, 17 Nov. 1857.

[25] *Daily Picayune*, 18 Nov. 1857.

[26] *Daily Picayune*, 7 Oct. 1857.

[27] New Orleans *Daily Crescent*, 2 Feb. 1861.

[28] New Orleans *Daily True Delta*, 11 Jan. 1863.

[29]Wittke, p. 120.

[30]On the origins of minstrelsy, see Carl Wittke's *Tambo and Bones* and Langston Hughes and Milton Meltzer's *Black Magic* (Englewood Cliffs, N.J.: Prentice-Hall, 1967).

[31]Henry Whitney Bellows, *The Relation of Public Amusements to Public Morality* (New York: n.p., 1857), p. 16.

George David Coulon:
A Nineteenth Century French Louisiana Painter

JUDITH HOPKINS BONNER

Nineteenth century New Orleans attracted a number of artists seeking to establish their fortunes and reputations. The foundling settlement, after a mere hundred years development, was yet unable to support adequately these aspiring artists. Thus many remained for only a short period of time, or made occasional or seasonal visits to the city. Those artists fortunate enough to survive for any extended length of time are few. One such person was George David Coulon, who arrived from France as a small boy in 1833, began his artistic career in 1839, and thrived in his profession until he died in 1904. On achieving substantial financial success sufficient to support a family, he married Marie-Paoline Casbergue, a native Orleanean who was also an artist. The couple's talent later extended to their children, George Amédé and Emma, and for almost ninety years Coulon and his family made a considerable contribution to the culture of this then Creole city, which suffered through yellow fever and cholera epidemics, a Civil War, and Reconstruction, all during his lifetime.

George David Coulon's tenacity in pursuing his artistic interests despite his father's initial objections and the natural insecurity of such a profession makes his ultimately successful career significant. He became prominent in his lifetime and esteemed for his achievements. Of the Coulon family, he is the most important figure. His wife's artistic career was secondary to her wifely and maternal responsibilities, and his son and daughter never achieved his stature.

Coulon became thoroughly assimilated into the community and functioned as an integral part in its artistic activities. A student of local art instructors, Coulon in turn became an art teacher offering both private lessons and courses in educational institutions. His commissions included the decoration of public buildings, religious and charitable institutions, theaters, and annual celebrations such as parades. He was moderately versatile in his accomplishments, and his subject matter included portraiture, landscapes, genre and animal life, religious subjects and stage settings. He came to maturity of style early in his career and his development can be associated with his various activities, in particular his work with photography.

Coulon began to restore paintings as early as 1845, which increased his knowledge of materials and techniques. His work in making death masks for posthumous portraits certainly contributed to his sense of proportion, depth and transition of planes, and to the accuracy of his drawing. His having assisted the photographer John Hawley Clarke in the hand-painting of photographs profoundly increased his technical skills. Having kept a file of visual source material, he learned from the compositional work of other artists and photographers, including Harry Fenn, Ernest Ciceri, Constant-Joseph Brochart, and Toussaint Bigot, one of his former teachers.

Coulon's interests extended to other artists as well as to tangentially related fields. He assisted in the establishment of the Southern Art Union and its successor, the Artists' Association of New Orleans, where he was teacher of the elementary and drawing classes. An antiquarian and amateur naturalist, he collected gems, minerals and shells on his travels in the western hemisphere, and a note and drawing in the Louisiana State Museum reflect his curiosity about unusual fish in this region.

George David Coulon, having a deep sense of history, briefly recorded an account of artists who had visited or lived in the city of New Orleans. He also recorded his own familial background, training, and career in a three-page autobiography written for his fellow artist and collector Bror A. Wikstrom.[1] With this letter, dated 4 March 1901, he made one of the first attempts to recount the history of art in New Orleans.[2]

The son of a watchmaker, he was born in Seloncourt (Doubs) France, on 14 November 1822. By his own account, he was instinctively drawn toward art as a young child, making drawings and coloring them with indigo and the juice of herbs and berries. His father, George Louis Coulon, brought his wife, daughter, and four sons to New Orleans in the summer of 1833.[3] George was ten years of age at this time and remained in New Orleans for nearly seventy-one years until his death on 28 February 1904, at the age of eighty-one.[4]

The Coulon family first appeared in New Orleans during a period of expansion and economic growth—only thirty years after the Louisiana Purchase. The reason for their immigration is unknown. Although there were other Coulons who were listed as residents in the city previous to their arrival, any family relationship remains sketchy. George Louis Coulon successfully established himself as a watchmaker.[5] Although George David Coulon writes that his mother died soon after their arrival, the exact date of her death is uncertain.[6]

During this period of growth the need for free public education necessitated the formation of the city's first institution for public education—at the Old Convent on Condé Street.[7] In 1836, Coulon attended that school, where he also received his first formal training in drawing and painting under Toussaint Bigot. According to Coulon, Bigot had studied in the "first schools of France" and with Baron Watelet and J. Louis David, and had arrived in New Orleans in 1816.[8] Having taught at Rennes, Brittany, he established himself in New Orleans as a drawing teacher. When the first public school was formed in 1836, Bigot was employed as its first teacher, Professor of the Primary and Drawing Schools, and was assisted by an English teacher.[9] Young George David was one of the first pupils of this school. That he was the last surviving student was cited in his obituary notice for its historical significance.[10]

Sometime before or after he left school, George David also "took lessons" with François (Frantz) Fleishbein,[11] the portrait painter. Whether Fleishbein was on the staff at the public school is not known, but Coulon probably studied with Fleishbein after receiving his father's permission to study art as a profession. The young lad's interest was so persevering that after he left school his father's attempt to have him follow in the watchmaking profession failed in

favor of his own interests—or as Coulon defined it, his "natural
inclination." One obituary notice states that "left to earn his own
living, when quite a small boy, Mr. Coulon began the study and
practice of art when 18 years of age."[12] This statement, certainly
drawn on the hazy memory of Coulon's comments to his family, is
not quite accurate for our own historical interests. Although he
began to "practice" his art at about eighteen years of age, his study
of art began at age sixteen while he was still living at home with his
father. Coulon himself recounts the events of his early years for
Wikstrom: "After leaving school, Father tried to make me learn his
profession (watchmaker) but after a few months trial, he decided to
let me follow my natural inclination, and about 1838 I learned
Decoration painting with Antonio Mondelli Sen." This provided
his first monumental break, and it is surely through this connection
that he became an assistant to Léon Pomarède, the son-in-law of
Mondelli.

For over one hundred years, St. Louis Cathedral had been the
only church serving the Catholic community in New Orleans, and
prayers, songs and homilies were given in the French language of
the majority of inhabitants of the Old Quarter of the city. The
population in the late 1830s included a large number of Americans
and Irish immigrants, and the city had been expanded to include
the American sector. A small makeshift church served this group of
citizens. It was therefore a truly momentous occasion to have a
second church, St. Patrick's, constructed in the city. The three
paintings above the altar in this church are monumental in size.
Allowed his choice of subject matter, Pomarède chose to copy
Raphael's well-known *Transfiguration* for the central painting.
By Coulon's own account, he assisted Pomarède with this central
mural. The full extent of his contribution to this painting is unde-
fined; however, it differs in depth of color, style, and execution
from the paintings which hang on either side. Although the painting does not approach the graceful figures, subtle chiaroscuro, and
technical ability of Raphael, it was an ambitious undertaking for the
two young Frenchmen, and is passably successful. The paintings
were well received at the time and newspaper editorials were
exuberantly laudatory.[13] They are impressive in their sheer size

alone, and the accolades of the artists' contemporaries were well deserved for the extraordinary accomplishment.

At this point in his autobiography, Coulon mentions assisting with the fresco on the ceiling of the Old Criminal Court in the Cabildo, although he does not establish specifically that it was Pomarède whom he assisted or that it was at this time. In addition to these recollections on his apprenticeship, Coulon gave the following account of his formal training:

> In the later part of 40 I took lessons in portrait painting with Julien Hudson. Born in this city, he was a pupil of Abel de Pujol of Paris: After I again took lessons of figure and landscape painting with T. Bigot, and at the end of 41 painted a small portrait for Italy that gave me much satisfaction.
> I then studied animals, flowers, and still life, In 1842 I painted my second portrait. I kept on painting a quantity of human heads.

This passage clearly indicates Coulon's feeling for his training. He records the detail as precisely as he can remember the events which occurred sixty years earlier. His interests as a young artist were ambitious and eclectic. In order to feel his instruction complete, he included in his training the study of portraiture, landscape, animals, flowers, and still life. His desire to record his teachers and give biographical information regarding their training and experience manifests his satisfaction with having trained under their direction. Although he continued to study with Jacques Amans and other artists throughout his lifetime,[14] he obviously felt that he had concluded his formal schooling. His own comment regarding the "small portrait for Italy that gave me much satisfaction" reveals that he was pleased with the instruction he had received as well as with his own efforts.

This 1841 portrait is unknown; the second portrait is in all probability the *Boy With a Rose* in the collection of the Louisiana State Museum (*Figure 1*). Dated 1842, the painting is an admirable first attempt for the twenty-year-old artist. Painted according to the prevailing taste for Neo-classicism, the boy is seen against a colossal column in a half-length formal pose. The palette is limited and somber and the light areas differ dramatically from the dark shadowing behind the child. The face and hands are less than

Figure 1. Boy With a Rose, signed "G. D. Coulon, 1842." Oil on canvas, 22″ x 18″ (55.9 x 45.7 cm). From the Collection of the Louisiana State Museum. Photograph courtesy of the Louisiana State Museum.

convincing in their lack of roundness and in the limp skeletal
support of the hand.

Coulon began to experience a measure of success quite early, and
by 1845 he found additional employment in restoration work,
which implies that his craftsmanship was respected by the local
citizenry. In his autobiography he states, "Since 1845 I have re-
lined and restored a large quantity of paintings." Further financial
support came from commissions for paintings for civic and church
and charitable institutions. The only other painting for which
Coulon gives a date in his autobiographical letter is that of a *Wor-
shipping of the Shepherds*, painted in 1848. The painting was
large, approximately eight feet by six feet, and according to Coulon
was still in 1901 at the "Montegut St. Asylum." This large composition reveals a marked improvement in development. The compli-
cated compositional arrangement, the lighting, tonal modeling, and
rich coloring attest to his developing technical skills. It is this painting which first hints at Coulon's nonconformity to the norm. The
Virgin is depicted as a blue-eyed blonde; Joseph leans an elbow on
the back of a cow, his index finger crooked across his upper lip as
he skeptically surveys the scene before him; the shepherds are
dressed in what appears to be Flemish clothing; and women take a
prominent part in the adoration of the child rather than serving in
the capacity of midwife, angel, or allegorical figure. A partially visible angel flying above (the canvas has been cut down) strews
camellia-shaped flowers on the infant.

Coulon at this time was living at 47 Condé Street, which is
given in the *New Orleans City Directories* as his address from 1846
through 1848. An earlier listing given in 1843 is that of a C. D.
Coulon at 20 Jefferson. This is in all probability a typographical
error as no other painter of that name appears before or after 1843.
However since George David Coulon is not included in the 1844
and 1845 directories, this cannot be ascertained. In 1849, he is
listed as J. D. Coulon, portrait painter at 83 Condé. For the next
six years, from 1850 to 1856, his address is given as 103 Condé
Street. This stability of address suggests that he had met with
measurable success as a painter. Certainly his marriage in 1850 to
an eighteen-year-old French girl, Marie-Paoline (called Paoline),

had some bearing on this stability, whether as an outcome of
success, or as an influence on him. By 1857, within seven years of
his marriage, he moved to the corner of Claiborne and Laharpe
where he lived for the remainder of his life.[15] Of his two surviving
children, George Amédé was born on 28 July 1854, and Mary Elizabeth Emma (called Emma) was born on 11 May 1859.[16]

From his youthful obstinacy regarding the direction of his career,
Coulon seems to have exhibited tendencies toward deliberateness,
carefulness, and distinctiveness. Throughout his life he remained
tenacious and determined. It seems logical, in light of his age that
he married and began his family only after his future appeared
secure or at least promising. Coulon was twenty-seven years old,
and nearly twelve years had elapsed since he embarked upon his
career as an artist. In 1851, the year following his marriage, Coulon
began to "give lessons of drawing and painting in young Ladies
Institutions," which he continued to do through 1865. Obviously
by this time his standing in the community was such that he
secured employment under the auspices of local teaching estab-
lishments.

In 1854 Coulon is cited in the *Courrier,* a local newspaper, as a
"finished artist" for having done at least six banners representing
the various fire companies in the 17th Annual Firemen's Parade.[17]
In the city which had twice earlier experienced disastrous fires that
destroyed it, the anniversary of the establishment of the Fire De-
partments was celebrated on a grand scale, with a procession of
thirty to forty companies of firemen through the principal streets
accompanied by a brass band. Their machines were decorated with
streamers and flowers, while one engine was even mounted on a
wheeled platform drawn by a team of twelve horses. The newspaper account was exuberant in its praise of the event, using such
terms as "great taste and gorgeous manner" and included among
the processing firemen "judges, physicians, lawyers, &c.—men
who are filling the first offices of our city and parishes." Expressing
appreciation for the generosity of the volunteer-protectors, the writer claims Coulon as "our own young Creole artist," although he was
not technically of "Creole" origin. The observation regarding his
skillful execution, design, and use of coloring specifies that Coulon

was considered to be a "finished" artist by the populace. The painting of the banners reveals, however, the wide variety of artistic
endeavors in which an artist had to be facile in order to support
himself.

Coulon states in his autobiography that "until about 1853 all the
portraits I made I painted them direct from Nature and from Death
Masks, I painted about 100 portraits from masks that I took after
Death." This curious statement seems to mean that after 1853 he
also painted portraits from photographs. This comment points up
the intense need for the families of the deceased to capture a final
image of the lost loved one. The vast number of commissions to
perform this morose task is not necessarily limited to pre-1853
portraits by Coulon.

One of the portraits listed by Coulon in his autobiography is that
of Rev. James Ignatius Mullon,[18] the founder of St. Patrick's
Church. The painting was probably executed after the death of
Father Mullon in 1866, or shortly before that year, and is possibly
done after a photograph. Well loved by the citizenry, Father Mullon became more endeared to New Orleanians because of his con-
frontations with General Benjamin "Beast" Butler, commander of
the Federal troops which occupied the city. Mullon's reputation
was one of generosity to all denominations and his "parish" extended beyond its appointed limits.

Our knowledge of Coulon's activities in the years immediately
following the Civil War are sketchy; there are few surviving paintings from this period in comparison with his later output. Judging
from subsequent newspaper articles, one surmises that he must
have continued with a fair amount of work and enjoyed a reputation
of some success, for he is referred to as "the eminent artist" or "that
accomplished artist."[19] After he discontinued teaching painting
and drawing in "young Ladies Institutions," he continued to give
lessons privately. An article in the *Daily Picayune* in 1871 describes a young sixteen-year-old boy named John Kingston, who
lived in Coulon's district, and who had taken "but 25 lessons (from
Mr. Coulon) in painting."[20] This article is revelatory in several
ways. It indicates avenues of art activities for Coulon as teacher and
Kingston as a youthful beginner competing at a State Fair. It also

reveals a skill which exceeds the talent of the average pupil Kingston's age and the resultant success of the capable student and teacher. Additionally, the youth's handling of color is cited as being particularly impressive for a student of his age. Coulon himself considered color important, and in his notes on "Old Painters in New Orleans," he is critical of Salazar for not being a good colorist while he cites Rheinhardt as "a rich colorist" and an artist by the surname of Carter as being a "good Colorist." This criterion, which he considered important in 1901, he obviously considered essential throughout his life, in his own work and that of his students. His emphasis on color in portraiture was apparently a common interest with the citizenry of the time.

In 1872 Coulon collaborated with the photographer John Hawley Clarke to produce pastel and oil-colored photographs. Their advertisements offer this "new and beautiful style of pastels, or colored photographs . . . brought to the very perfection of the photographic art."[21] While this advertisement promises a blend of "durability and saliency of feature and expression," another promises that "nothing is left untouched by the artist's brush which tends to portray all the prominent features of the original."[22]

The development of the daguerreotype and the following improvements in the camera created a dilemma for artists. The populace not only desired the greater realism in their portraiture; they were equally appreciative of the frugality of expense and time provided by the camera. The desire for capturing the nearly exact replica of the image of a loved one, however, fell short in the photographs in a major aspect—that of color. The mind and eye perceived the human image in color; therefore, the photographs were tinted quite early after the development of the daguerreotype.[23] Inevitably, the photographs were colored with pastel and watercolors and oil paints, uplifting the photographic process into a "higher art." Although Coulon was fifty years old at the time of his short-lived association with Clarke, his work was directly affected by the experience. His figures began to take on greater volume and roundness, his accuracy in drawing was further improved, his ability to render subtle facial contours and gradations of shadow increased. It is precisely in this respect that Coulon's later works suffer from a loss of the spontaneity and liveliness found in his earlier works. With his increased technical skills came a profoundly pronounced ability to portray the detail of clothing and jewelry. His reputation grew accordingly, and he is still remembered for the jewel-like execution of detail in his portraiture. This was a pitfall not unique to Coulon, and one is reminded of Giorgio Vasari's sixteenth century warning that "excessive study or diligence tends to produce a dry style when it becomes an end in itself."[24] Gradually, this interest in detail produced a general flattening of the figure as Coulon executed patterns on the already flat surface of the canvas.

Coulon's progression of style can be readily seen in the comparison of his earliest known portrait, *Boy With a Rose*, 1842, and the portrait of Anthony Rasch, the silversmith, which was painted in the 1850s (*Figure 2*). In the latter his drawing and understanding of anatomy are secure; his handling of color and chiaroscuro skillful; and his brushwork accurate yet freely applied. A later portrait, *Emma Sarah Hulm Everett*, 1891, retains some vitality of brushwork in the facial highlights, but the richly brocaded jacket and blouse receive equal attention, thus the work becomes a portrait of clothing and status as much as a physical likeness of the sitter (*Figure 3*). Coulon executed eleven portraits for the Everett family from 1891 through 1893, and his skill comes to its full fruition in the portrait of the youngest child, *Emma Agnes Everett Vulliet Coleman ("Popsy")*, painted in 1893 (*Figure 4*). Coulon masterfully renders the detail and delicacy of the lace dress and harmoniously balances the tension between the richness of detail of the garment's white-on-white patterning and the captured facial expression. The artistic treatment is dextrous in drawing, modeling, and coloring. The tone, value, and intensity of color are finely controlled. The child still holds a flower, as does the *Boy With a Rose* painted fifty-one years earlier, but the fleshy hand is now credible in the underlying system of bones and their junctures. The floral arrangement is as crisply delineated as a botanical illustration; the background vegetation becomes more hazy with distance, as is characteristic of all Coulon works.

Coulon's fascination with detail and patterning has its roots in his

Figure 2. Portrait of Anthony Rasch, signed "G. Coulon." (Undated). Oil on wood, 12″ x 9 3/4″ (30.5 x 24.8 cm). Private collection, New Orleans, La. Photograph courtesy of the Historic New Orleans Collection.

Figure 3. Portrait of Emma Sarah Hulm Everett, signed "G. D. Coulon, 1891." Oil on canvas, 24″ x 20″ (61 x 50.8 cm). Private collection, New Orleans, La. Photograph by Judy Cooper.

Figure 4. Portrait of Emma Agnes Everett Vulliet Coleman ("Popsy") signed "G. D. Coulon/93." Pastel on paper, 33″ x 27″ (33.8 x 68.6 cm). Private collection, New Orleans, La. Photograph by Judy Cooper.

earliest art activities and training. As a child he was accustomed to seeing his father carefully synchronize the minute and delicately balanced inner mechanisms of watches. He certainly accepted the idea that his father's work was time consuming, requiring the utmost patience and painstaking care in order to insure a functioning product. His initial training in his father's profession would have reinforced this thought. Following his abortive attempt at watchmaking, he studied "Decoration painting" but it is not exactly clear what type "decoration" this was. Further, his experience in painting stage settings had an effect on his later works.

Nowhere is Coulon's methodical patience more evident throughout his lifetime than in his paintings of landscapes, which are almost always reminiscent of stage scenery (*Figure 5*). His keen powers of observation are immediately apparent. One has only to drive through the Louisiana countryside to realize his successful depiction of the land with its low horizons, wide expanses of land, and open skies with the wispy clouds which blow in from the Gulf of Mexico. His sense of the infinite variety of the Louisiana landscape is obvious, and there are no two landscapes which are alike in their compositions, as is often found in the works of Alexander J. Drysdale. Yet the works are unmistakably characteristic of George David Coulon, and even his unsigned landscapes are easily identifiable by amateur historians, collectors, and aficionados. There is always a distinct sense of mist and wetness, a hazy atmospheric distant background with hazy blue-greys and greyish-greens, detailed palmetto shrubbery and marsh grasses in the foreground, and graceful garlands of grey moss randomly scattered on frail cypress boughs or massive oak branches. He took delight in depicting the lacy effect of filigree-like foliage, the slight bend of branches made pliant under the gentle force of wind and rain, the patterns of overlapped leaves, and layers of shrubbery and trees. He subtly captures the melancholy appeal of the scattered and solitary cypress tree. Perhaps most appealing is his use of pure, unmuddied color in an endless variety of tones of green and blue. Accurate in value and color, he contrasts vibrant spring green and deep lush green with hazy grey and pale blue. One can readily imagine that his lyrical compositions were more easily discernible in the dim

Figure 5. Southern Landscape, signed "G. D. Coulon 87." Oil on canvas, 12 1/8″ x 20 3/16″ (30.8 x 51.3 cm). The Historic New Orleans Collection. Photograph courtesy of the Historic New Orleans Collection.

lighting of Victorian interiors than the dark moody landscapes of Richard Clague, William Buck, and Marshall Smith with their deep brown tones and coffee-colored swamp waters. Coulon's landscapes were constantly cited as being "jewel-like" and "little gems," and these works hold the same appeal today. In 1896 his contemporary, May W. Mount observed:

> Mr. Coulon is justly noted as a landscape painter and his delineations of Louisiana scenery are particularly effective and beautiful. There is always a charm about the atmospheric effects in Mr. Coulon's paintings, and a delicacy of touch and coloring that render them idyllic poems of nature. Mr. Coulon is one of the oldest and best known artists in New Orleans, and is numbered among the city's most successful teachers. His studios are filled with the excellent work which always attracts instant admiration at every exhibition.[25]

Coulon also did a series of studies of western landscapes, which differ somewhat in style, coloring, and lighting from his Louisiana scenery. There are still extant a significant number of these paintings, but it is his Louisiana landscapes which are better known and which helped to keep him afloat financially. In 1888, his son, George A. Coulon published a diary of his travel through the Atchafalaya Basin entitled "350 Miles in a Skiff Through the Louisiana Swamps." George David's placement of an advertisement in this publication assures us of his continued teaching and restoration work. The notice is stated in such a manner as to suggest that Coulon specialized in giving instructions on painting Louisiana landscapes, or at least that his paintings of Louisiana landscapes were a specialty which were worthy of specific note.

Mrs. Mount's 1896 text cites Coulon as "among the city's most successful teachers." There are, though, only six of his students whose names are known: John Kingston, Madeline Seebold Molinary, Marie de Jaham, Eloise Walker Duffy, Adine Reed and Carrie Trost, the last two of whom became art teachers in 1893.[26] By reputation Coulon was a kind and gentle instructor who frequently went to the homes of his students for lessons, as well as gave lessons at his own studio. His energy served him well, and he was able not only to support himself but to offer support, encouragement and instruction to other artists.

The post-war difficulties in the South are paralleled by the difficulties experienced by artists. In an 1881 article in the *Daily
Picayune,* an anonymous artist advocates elevating standards of
artworks and cites obstacles in obtaining models and difficulties in
obtaining commissions: "We have to restrict ourselves to certain
styles to suit popular taste, and a portrait painting is the only kind of
work that is remunerative."[27] This lament speaks eloquently for the
need of mutual support and aggressive promotion of the arts. Citing
wide support for music and drama, the artist mourns the meager
encouragement which painters received, and he observes that this
limited support was not forthcoming from the wealthy. He ap-
plauds the recent formation of an art society to encourage and
perpetuate art in the city of New Orleans. From its inception,
Coulon was a founding father of this society, called the Southern
Art Union, and was a member of its various committees as well as
an instructor in drawing. Others on the Teaching Art Committee
included William Buck, Achille Perelli, Andres Molinary, Paul
Poincy, T. S. Moise, Marshall Smith, and T. A. Cox.[28] There was
considerable interest in this organization and other members included Mary Ashley Townsend, John Genin, Charles Giroux, and
Edward Livingston. The group was rather lofty and ambitious in its
goals and included the fine arts, crafts, and needlework, claiming
"grand results in the formation of a practical Woman's Exchange, a
public library, an art gallery, lecture rooms and school of design."[29]
It merged with the "Women's Industrial Association" and for a time
managed to accommodate the interests of its various members. Art
classes met three days a week from 2:00 to 4:00 p. m. and teachers
received fifty percent of instruction fees, the remainder going to the
Art Union for the purchase of easels, plates, casts, and supplies.[30]

Although the Southern Art Union had but a short duration, lasting
from 1880 until sometime after 1883, it proved to be the embryo of
the Artists' Association of New Orleans, established in 1885, and
incorporated in 1886.[31] Coulon, sixty-three years of age at the time
and older than the majority of other artists involved in establishing
this society, was active at the beginning, although this activity
decreased in his later years. By the time the Artists' Association
merged with the Arts and Exhibition Club in 1903, becoming the

Art Association of New Orleans (which continues until the present day), Coulon was in ill health; he died the following year. His presence from the inception in these organizations to help other artists is in keeping with his past activities in art—painting, exhibiting, teaching.

Simultaneous with the establishment of the Artists' Association of New Orleans was the organization of the World's Industrial and Cotton Centennial Exposition in 1885 and 1886. The Exposition was conceived to draw attention to the state and its indigenous talent and products, thereby to stimulate the interest of the rest of the world and promote new opportunities. Although not proving the enormous success it was touted to become, the exposition did make some advances, especially in the area of the arts and letters. The flourishing of the arts obviously led to an increased market for paintings of landscapes, genre, and still life, and an increase in commissions for portraiture. It is in this period that Coulon seems to have done exceptionally well, for there is a larger surviving body of works for this later period. Although it is perfectly natural and predictable that an artist's later works have a greater rate of survival than the early works, it is nevertheless impressive that a man in his sixties and seventies could have been as productive as Coulon was. A series of portraits of Supreme Court Justices mentioned in his autobiography were executed from about 1885 through 1897. These, as well as the series of eleven portraits executed for the Everett family from 1891 through 1893, underscore the reputation Coulon had established by this period, as well as the obvious satisfaction of his patrons.

In 1901, when the seventy-eight year old Coulon briefly sketched his life for Wikstrom, he wrote that he was still painting "portraits, Landscapes, &c." His obituary notice verifies that he was industrious until the end; thus, we can assume that there was a market for his work at this time. This surely must have been a satisfactory feeling for a man who had had a definite interest in art from his youth and who had insisted on pursuing that interest despite its uncertain future in a still developing settlement in the "New World."

Coulon was so outstanding in his prodigious performance that the writer of one obituary observes, "He was a hard worker, always at his easel, and leaves many canvases behind."[32] His efforts and accomplishments paved the way for future artists who were to become privileged in choice of subject matter and in the development of their own style. Their work would reflect the freshness which comes from experimentation rather than experiencing the dryness which comes from repeating the formula of past successes. In this light, we can appreciate the laudatory notices which credit George David Coulon with being "the veteran artist" and "the Dean of Art Spirit in Louisiana," and which lament the passing of "another of the noted old landmarks."[33]

NOTES

[1]These documents are preserved by the Louisiana State Museum in its scrapbook on artists, Scrapbook No. 100, along with the original drawings and clippings from the Wikstrom scrapbook. All further quotations from Coulon's autobiography or his notes on "Old Painters in New Orleans" are found in these documents.

[2]W. Joseph Fulton and Roulhac B. Toledano, "New Orleans Landscape Painting of the Nineteenth Century," *Antiques*, 93 (April 1968), 505.

[3]Autobiography, Scrapbook No. 100. Unless otherwise noted, this letter is the source of any biographical information given.

[4]Obituary notices for George David Coulon include the following: *The Times Democrat*, 29 Feb. 1904, p. 2, col. 7, and p. 10, col. 4–5; *The Daily Picayune*, 29 Feb. 1904, p. 2, col. 1, and p. 6, col. 5., *The Daily Picayune*, 6 Mar. 1904, p. 6, col. 5; *The Times Democrat*, 6 Mar. 1904, p. 2, col. 4.

[5]*New Orleans City Directories, 1838–1866.*

[6]It was not uncommon at the time to neglect placing a notice of death of a woman in the local newspapers. Also, during times of epidemic, when great numbers of burials were hastily made, families frequently neglected making a public notice. Although there was an epidemic in the city in 1833, it cannot be ascertained that this was the cause of Mrs. Coulon's death, nor that her death occurred in the same year of her arrival.

[7]*The Courier*, 10 June 1841, p. 3, col. 5.

[8]Bigot was born in Rennes, France, circa 1794, and died in New Orleans on 14 Mar. 1869, after having lived in the city for 53 years. *The New Orleans Bee*, 17 Mar. 1869, p. 1, col. 5.

[9]*The Courier*, 10 June 1841, and *The Times Democrat*, 29 Feb. 1904.

[10]*The Times Democrat*, 29 Feb. 1904.

[11]Also spelled Fleischbein.

[12]*The Daily Picayune*, 29 Feb. 1904.

[13]*The Louisiana Courier* [spelled here with a single "r"] 9 Nov. 1841, p. 2, col. 2, by Alf. Latour-Allard; *The New Orleans Commercial Bulletin*, 26 Jan. 1843, p. 2, col. 4; see also Samuel Wilson, Jr., "The Building of St. Patrick's Church," in Roger Baudier, et al., *St. Patrick's of New Orleans: 1833–1958*, ed. Charles L. Dufour (New Orleans: St. Patrick's Parish, 1958), pp. 47–50.

[14]*The Times-Democrat*, 29 Feb. 1904. Although spelled "Amance" in the death notice, this is certainly Jacques Amans, who was in the city from about 1836 to 1856. See Mary Louise Tucker, "Jacques G. L. Amans (1801–88): Portrait Painter in Louisiana, 1836–56," Master's thesis, Tulane Univ., 1970.

[15]New Orleans City Directories, 1843–1904. The 1880 *Census* lists his real estate assets at $1500, and personal assets at $250; the 1900 *Census* lists Coulon as owning his own home, and after his death, Paoline and Emma continued to reside at this address until about 1911.

[16]Marie-Paoline Casbergue Coulon died 3 July 1914. *New Orleans Health Department, Death Certificates*, p. 1108, gives her age as "83 years and 19 days" at the time of death. Her birthdate therefore is 14 June 1831. The date of death for George Amédé is yet unknown, but it is probably circa 1922. His date of birth is found in *New Orleans Health Department, Birth Records*, XIV, 265. Emma was christened Mary Elizabeth Emma Coulon at St. Augustine Church on 11 June 1859. See *Register of Baptisms*, III, 144. She died on 1 Apr. 1928, and is buried with her parents in St. Louis Cemetery #3. *The Times-Picayune*, 3 Apr. 1928, Sec. I, p. 2, col. 8.

[17]*The Courrier*, Sunday, 5 Mar. 1854, p. 4, col. 1.

[18]Actually, Coulon lists two paintings of "Rev. F. Mullen" [sic]. One of these portraits hangs in St. Patrick's, the other is unknown.

[19]*The Daily Picayune*, 24 Nov. 1872, p. 11, col. 1; and *The National Republican*, 11 Dec. 1872, p. 4, col. 1.

[20]*The Daily Picayune*, 12 Jan. 1871, p. 1, col. 4.

[21]*The Daily Picayune*, 24 Nov. 1872.

[22]*The National Republican*, 11 Dec. 1872.

[23]Margaret Denton Smith, "Photography in New Orleans, 1840–1865," Master's thesis, Tulane Univ., 1977, p. 18.

[24]Giorgio Vasari, *The Lives of the Artists*, tr. by George Bull (Middlesex, England: Penguin, 1976), p. 251.

[25]May W. Mount, *Some Notables of New Orleans: Biographical and Descriptive Sketches of the Artists of New Orleans and Their Work* (New Orleans: n. p., 1896), p. 136.

[26]*The Daily Picayune*, 12 Jan. 1871, p. 1, col. 4; Herman de Bachelle Seebold, *Old Louisiana Plantation Homes and Family Trees* (Gretna, La: Pelican, 1971), I, 220; *The New Orleans Item*, 5 Oct 1916, p. 14, col. 2; Isaac Monroe Cline, *Contemporary Art & Artists in New Orleans* (New Orleans: n. p., 1924 [reprinted from Louisiana State Museum Biennal Report]), p. 7; and *The Times Democrat*, 11 June 1893, p. 3, col. 2.

[27]*The Daily Picayune*, 24 Mar. 1881, p. 2, col. 3.

[28]*The New Orleans Bee*, 16 Nov. 1881, p. 1, col. 5; and *The New Orleans Bee*, 4 May 1881, p. 4, col. 1.

[29]*The Daily Picayune*, 22 May 1881, p. 2, col. 4.

[30]*The New Orleans Democrat*, 12 May 1881, p. 8, col. 4.

[31]*Charter, Constitution and By Laws of the Artist's Association with a list of members* (New Orleans: Hopkins Printing, 1893), p. 3.

[32]*The Daily Picayune*, 29 Feb. 1904.

[33]*The Daily Picayune*, 29 Feb. 1904.

The Creole Architecture of Nineteenth Century New Orleans

EUGENE D. CIZEK

New Orleans at the beginning of the nineteenth century was one of America's richest and most unique cities. Her wealth came from the products of the large plantation and natural resource hinterland, the banking and merchandising enterprise of a growing region, the immense fortunes made by the eighteenth century colonists and the great port on the Mississippi River, which the rich imports and exports of middle America and an expanding nation created.

Her uniqueness initially came from the French and Spanish— Latin culture that built a city and an empire in the hot, humid, subtropical environment of South Louisiana. The great marshes and fertile farmlands were all part of a delicate ecological system that was governed by the Mississippi River, its Delta, and man's respectful and sensitive marriage with the conditions of nature.

The Latin colonists learned very quickly to adapt their preconceptions of Western Europe's architecture and life style to their new setting. They learned from the American Indians how to utilize not only their traditional foods and seasonings to create a new Creole cuisine, but also their time-tested methods of building materials and construction. The slaves brought their knowledge of African life, often from environments very similar to that of New Orleans, and showed great skill in applying their native abilities to the materials available for constructing colonial New Orleans.

The immigration of Caribbean colonists, especially those from the slave rebellions of Santo Domingo, added further knowledge and experience in creating an environmentally responsive architecture. Many of these Caribbean immigrants were free people of color who were master builders and craftsmen. They helped to create a cooperative system of apprenticeship that led to a unique kind of architecture, a blending of the best of all the cultures— Louisiana Creole architecture.

In early nineteenth century New Orleans, the Louisiana Purchase intensified an already dangerous rivalry between the aristocratic Creoles and the immigrating Americans. The Creoles' attitude toward work and the making and use of money did not fit the Americans' ideal that richer is better, that more is better, that bigger is better and that the local sense of history and culture is only a stumbling block to progress, particularly as defined by the Americans. New Orleans was still culturally and socially a Creole City, and the early Americans did their best to become an integral part of the established society, to marry into the original founding families and in a sense to become "Creole."

Although the Americans eventually triumphed in their control of money, New Orleans' Creole culture made a lasting impact throughout the nineteenth century. The primary influence is found in the residential architecture of the city. The same environmental factors which made steeply pitched roofs necessary to dispel the torrential rains of the region, the wide galleries to condition air and light and create outdoor living areas, did not change over time. Shaded balconies and patios also conditioned the hot, humid environment; French doors and long windows allowed the air to circulate at cooling floor levels; batten and louvered shutters gave protection from intruders as well as inclement weather and intense heat and sunlight. The need for these special architectural features resulted in the initial Creole architectural form and the subsequent international and national styles that were to become a part of the city.

From an architectural historian's viewpoint, one can develop a nomenclature for New Orleans' architecture that begins with Colonial and is followed by Creole, Greek Revival, Italianate Second Empire, Victorian, Edwardian and other special classical variations found in nineteenth century architecture. On the other hand, one could also preface each succeeding major style with "Creole," which perhaps best describes both the style and the culture represented at any one time. Because of the recognized and accepted needs to maintain the Creole in each later style, especially in residential architecture, one does not find the pure and American interpretations of the styles as established primarily by the eastern American academic and critical establishment. The distinctive Creole quality produced the unique form of nineteenth century New Orleans.

The drawings included here are shown in two series. The first series was developed as part of a study to establish guidelines for an "adaptive architecture"—a contemporary Creole architecture that would take account of urban patterns, the lessons of history, and New Orleans' natural environment. The second series is from the author's "Faces of New Orleans Collection." By studying the details and notations on the drawings, one can better understand the special qualities that are found in the Creole architecture of New Orleans. The wisdom of the original potpourri of cultures that created a lasting Creole cuisine also created a sensitivity to Creole residential development that survived throughout the nineteenth century and, one hopes, continues to survive.

Creole
Architecture

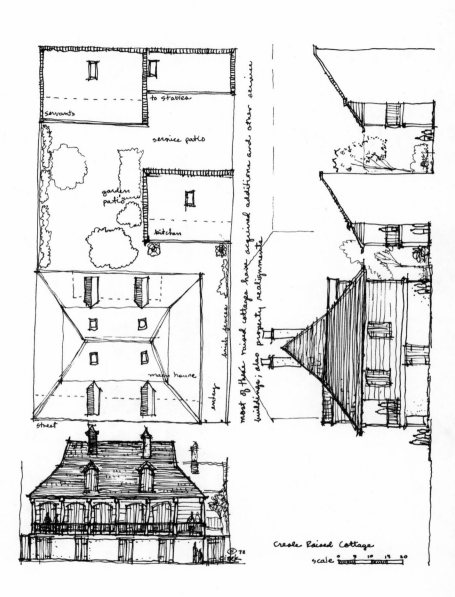

to stables

servants

service patio

garden patio

kitchen

main house

entry

street

brick fence w screen

most of these raised cottage have acquired additions and other service buildings; also property realignments

Creole Raised Cottage

scale 0 5 10 15 20

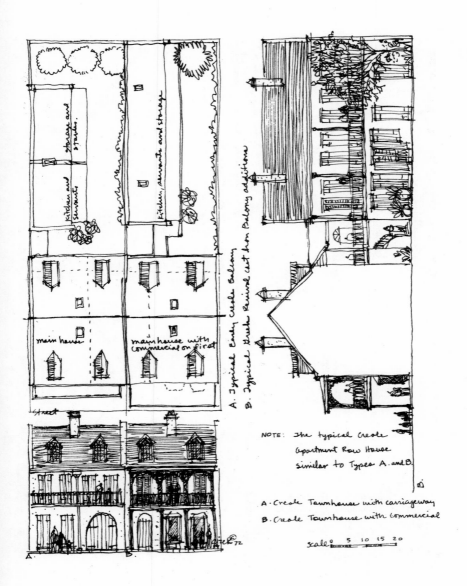

kitchen and servants

storage and studio.

kitchen, servants and storage

main house

main house with commercial on first

street

A.

B.

A. Typical Early Creole Saloon

B. Typical Greek Revival cut from Palomy additions

NOTE: The typical Creole Apartment Row House similar to Types A. and B.

A. Creole Townhouse with carriageway

B. Creole Townhouse with commercial

scale 0 5 10 15 20

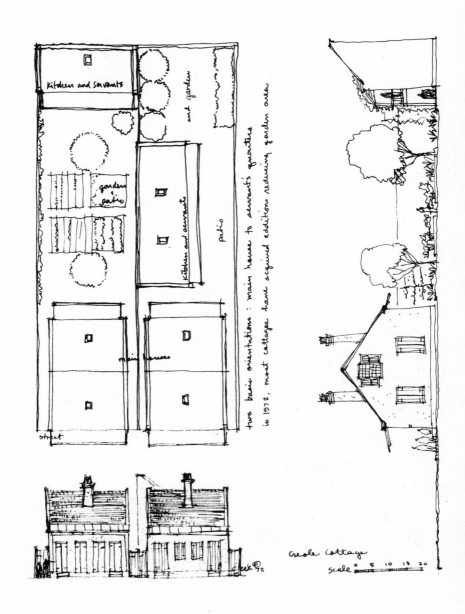

kitchen and servants

art garden

garden & patio

kitchen and servants

patio

main houses

street

two basic orientations: main house to servant's quarters in 1572, most cottages have acquired additions reducing garden area

creole cottage

scale 0 5 10 15 20

Greek 72

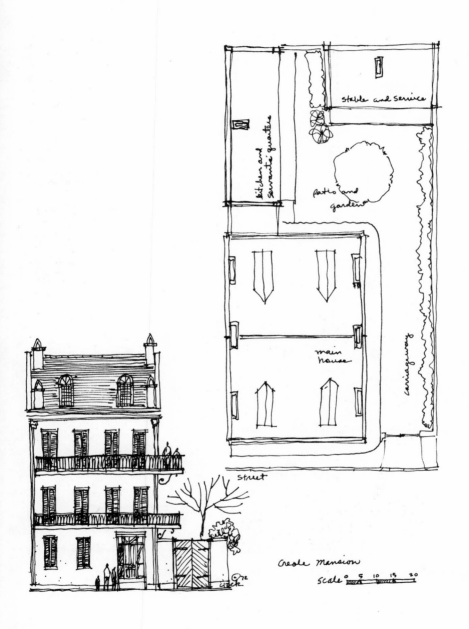

Stable and service

kitchen and servants quarters

patio and garden

main house

carriageway

street

Creole Mansion

Scale 0 5 10 15 20

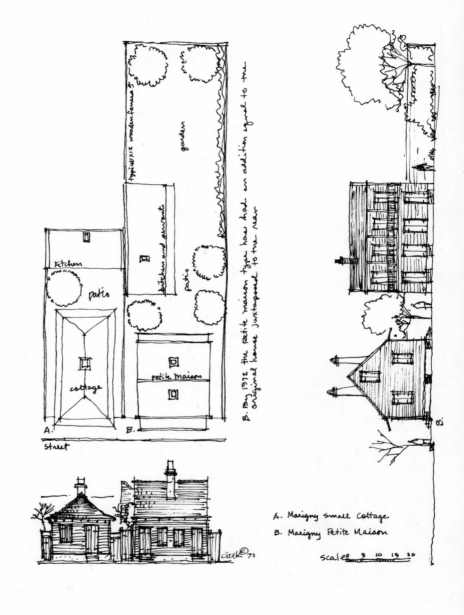

typical 2x12 wooden fence

garden

kitchen and servants

patio

Kitchen

patio

kitchen and servants

cottage

petite maison

A.

B.

Street

B. May 1972 the petite maison type has had an addition again to the original house juxtaposed to the rear

A. Marigny Small Cottage

B. Marigny Petite Maison

Scale 0 5 10 15 20

B.

Ceek © 72

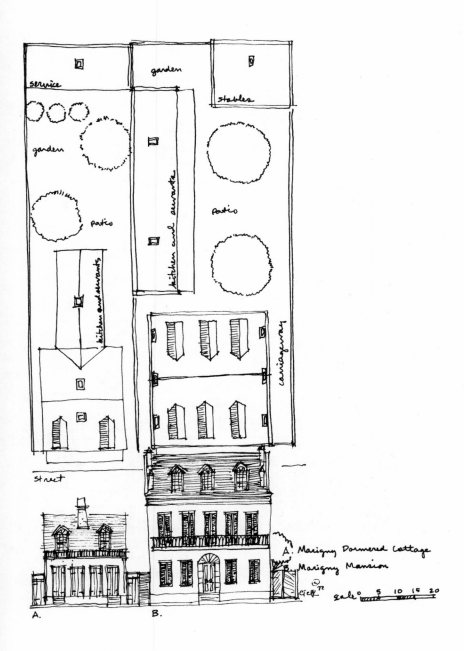

service

garden

stables

garden

patio

patio

kitchen and servants

kitchen and servants

carriageway

Street

A. Marigny Dormered Cottage
B. Marigny Mansion

CJCR '72

scale 0   5   10   15   20

A.   B.

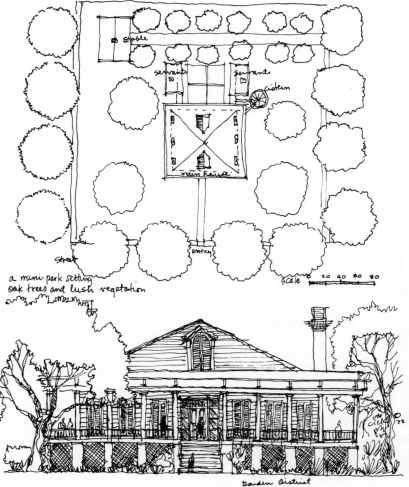

Stable

servants   servants

cistern

main house

Street   entry

a mini-park setting
oak trees and lush vegetation

Scale 0 20 40 60 80

Garden District

Early Plantation Mansion

Scale 0   5   10   15   20

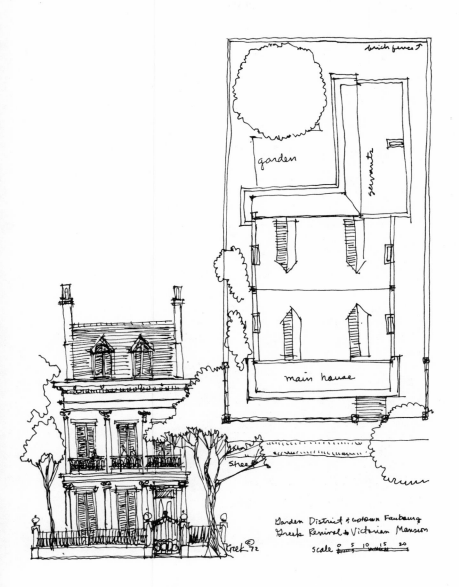

brick fence ⸗

garden

servants

main house

Greek '72

Garden District & uptown Faubourg
Greek Revival & Victorian Mansion
scale 0 5 10 15 20

Street

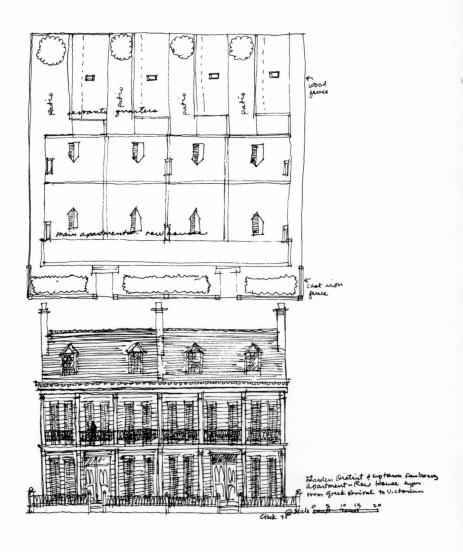

Patio

servants quarters

Patio

Patio

Patio

← wood fence

main apartments - row houses

← cast iron fence

Garden District & uptown Faubourg
Apartment - Row House types
& from Greek Revival to Victorian

0   5   10   15   20
@ scale

Cizek 78

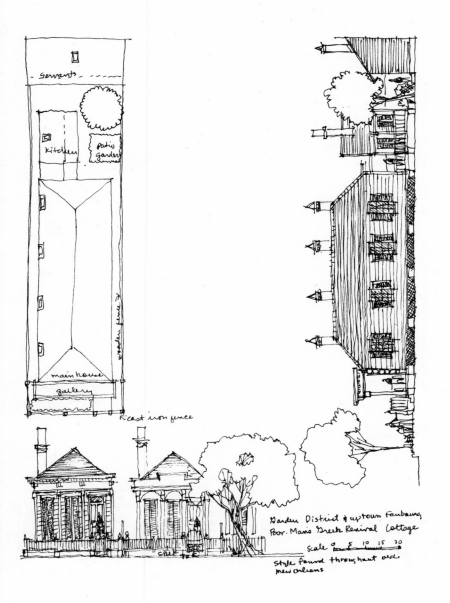

Servants

kitchen

patio
garden

wooden fence

main house

gallery

↑ cast iron fence

creek

Garden District & uptown Faubourg
Poor Man's Greek Revival Cottage

Scale 0   5   10   15   20

Style found throughout old
new orleans

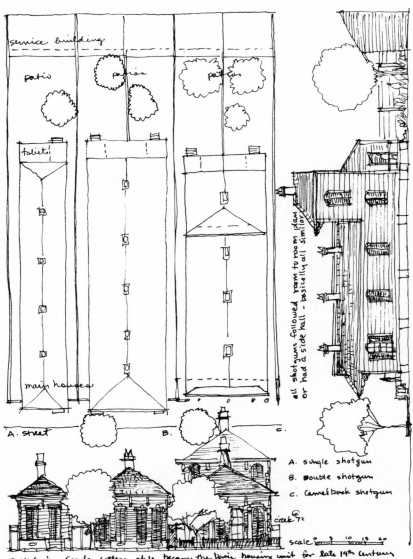

service building

patio   patio   patio

toilet's

all shotguns followed room to room plan
or had a side hall - basically all similar

main houses

A. street   B.   c.

A. single shotgun
B. double shotgun
c. camelback shotgun

creek '72

scale 5 10 15 20

The Victorian Creole cottage style became the basic housing unit for late 19th centuries
New Orleans

Faces
of
New Orleans

Napoleon House
late eighteenth century New Orleans
nome ot Mayor Girod

Chartres street

Creek August 1976©

Madame John's Legacy
Dumaine Street
an Eighteenth Century Dwelling

Cizek 71 ©

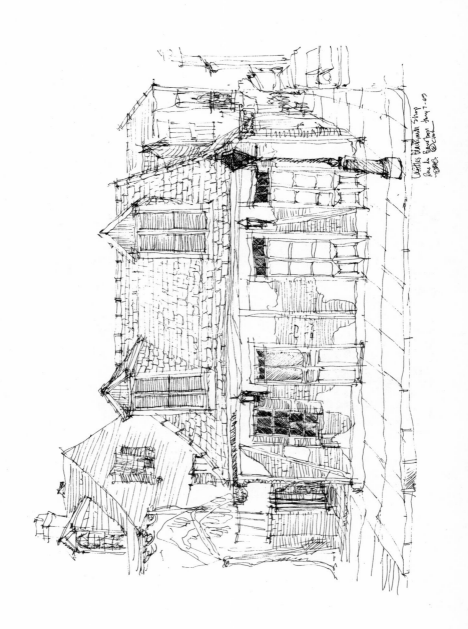

Charles Wadsworth Shop
Rue de Bourbon Aug 7-07
DBC ©2007

Gallier Hall 1845-1850. as viewed from Lafayette Square
architect - James Gallier, Jr.
became City Hall in 1853

1700-02 Carondelet · corner Euterpe Street   Czik '74
A Classic Style Double House with brocketed cornices

1519 Carondelet . Victorian Jigsaw House. Gizk '74

1139 Dryades - Church of St. John the Baptist and Expressway - click 74

2600 Block LaSalle c Fourth Street
Victorian Camelback Shotgun

Ark. 7r

St. Charles Avenue Street car
at Audubon Place
Late Nineteenth Century — current

Cizek 71

The Singing Heart:
A Study of the Life and Work of Pearl Rivers

W. KENNETH HOLDITCH

The old building still stands in downtown New Orleans, a narrow structure squeezed into the middle of a block. Once it was topped by a stone eagle perched on a globe, but now that is gone, along with the newspaper which it symbolized. The *Daily Picayune* has long since been swallowed up by a national newspaper syndicate, its individualistic identity enveloped by the anonymity of the modern medium. The building—in the past they called it "the old lady of Camp Street"; even buildings had character then—remains, dwarfed now by glistening but undistinguished skyscrapers on all sides, looking a bit like some antiquated maiden aunt who, though she may have outstayed her welcome, remains erect and proud.

It was 1876, in one of the offices of that Camp Street building, that a strange and memorable meeting took place between a group of newspaper men and a young woman. She was, as one contemporary commentator was later to describe her, "a slender, soft-voiced little woman,"[1] small of stature, with tiny hands; rather shy and retiring, she was nevertheless strong of will, and she had called the employees of the *Daily Picayune* together to make an announcement. She went into that meeting as a widow of twenty-seven, surely a bit frightened; but when she emerged from the room that day, she had become the first woman publisher of a major newspaper in all the country. Her name was Eliza Poitevent Holbrook, but she was better known to the world as Pearl Rivers.

Eliza Jane Poitevent was born in south Mississippi near the Louisiana state line 11 March 1849. Her father, Captain W. J. Poitevent, descendant of a French Huguenot family, was in the lumber business. Because of the illness of her mother, Eliza was reared for the most part by an aunt and uncle on their plantation near the Pearl River. Biographers report that she was the only white child for miles around in the sparsely settled area, and as a result spent a lonely adolescence. In later life she often remarked upon this sense of aloneness as a part of her character, regrettable but inescapable. This very state, however, no doubt contributed in large degree to her becoming a poet, a fact she herself acknowledges in "The Singing Heart":

> God made my heart a singing heart,
>   Because he knew that I
> Would be a creature set apart
>   For pain or pleasures high.[2]

Loneliness and isolation are recognized as blessings, marks of a special character, that of the poet; and being solitary, she came to live, as is often the case with an only child, a life of the imagination. The long hours wandering alone on the plantation, in the woods, the horseback rides in the surrounding countryside, developed in her a deep love of nature as well as a keen eye to observe its detail. In one of the few personal references in her poetry, she remarks that as a girl,

> I roamed the piny woods
> With heart as wild and step as free
> As roving Robin Hood's. (p. 120)

With animals, domestic and wild, and plants of all kinds she came to feel a closeness reflected in poem after poem. "I am March's own dear child," she announces in one cheerful lyric, "Just as weird and just as wild." Describing herself as "a fair-haired gypsy," she asserts that "the early roses know me," and so she wanders among her friends, the other "March Freaks," as the poem's title identifies them (p. 65). She came to feel as well a sense of communion even with inanimate objects—a familiar response for those who are much alone. In later years she was loath to throw away anything—a paper bag, an empty box, a piece of ribbon or string—lest it be "lonely" as she.[3]

Eliza turned to poetry, both the reading and the writing of it, at an early age, probably when she was about fourteen. Her education at the Amite Female Seminary, from which she graduated 5 July 1867, was spotty at best. She was later to observe that she "learned nothing that was of much use to me as a woman" and in 1888 to criticize what she labeled the "useless education" available for women in that day.[4] Some familiarity with the typical collection of books found in Southern homes in the mid-nineteenth century (the Bible, sets of Dickens and Scott, perhaps a few anthologies of "inspirational" poetry) makes it possible for one to guess the kind of reading material available to her. The newspapers she was exposed to, including the New Orleans *Daily Picayune*, often printed verse, but it was likely to be of the Emmeline Grangerford variety. Given these limitations, it is amazing that she should have written poetry at all, even further, that it should have had any artistic value, and finally that this teenaged girl from rural Mississippi should have known how to get it published.

That she was, as a critic once remarked of another isolated woman poet of the time, Emily Dickinson, "innocent of prosody," Eliza herself acknowledges in the poem which serves as Preface to her 1873 *Lyrics:*

> I never spent a single day
>   Learning the rules of art;
> Unconsciously my fingers play
>   The music of my heart. (p. 5)

As a result, her poetry is at times, especially in the early years, naive; but after all, she states, "I only sing of simple things/In simpler words than all" (p. 6). What she knew of the mechanism of versification she derived from her reading, however limited it may have been in scope (though surely not in volume). Her debt to the English Romantics and some of their American followers is observable in the early poetry and will be examined subsequently. In later years when she turned to more complex forms and subject matter in such works as "Hagar" and "Leah," it was again the benefits of reading other poets that provided her with what "rules of art" her creative urge required.

For some reason—whim or desire for anonymity or family pressure—she adopted a pseudonym, calling herself as poet Pearl

Rivers, a tribute to that stream which meandered through the landscape of her youth and for which she would in 1879 create in poetry
a legend. She submitted verse to the New York *Journal,* to New
Orleans newspapers, and to *South,* a literary magazine, and gained
immediate acceptance. John W. Overall, editor of *South,* which was
published in New Orleans, became a mentor for the young poet, a
service she acknowledged in 1873 by including him among the
"Three Singers" to whom *Lyrics,* her one published book, was
"Affectionately Dedicated."

It was during a visit to her grandfather, Samuel P. Russ, in New
Orleans in the late 1860s, that Eliza Poitevent met Colonel Alva
Morris Holbrook, publisher of the *Daily Picayune,* thereby changing her life and the history of newspapers in the Crescent City.
Holbrook, quite obviously charmed by the small and dainty young
woman, not only published her poetry but shortly thereafter offered
her a position as literary editor for his newspaper at a salary of
twenty-five dollars a week. Members of her family were doubtless
scandalized; a young Southern lady of breeding did not take a
business position, especially not in the rowdy world of newspapermen; bad enough that she should write and publish poetry.

Life was changing for Southerners in those days of deprivation
following the four years of disastrous and destructive warfare. Both
men and women in the South found themselves in occupations they
would have spurned before 1861. The story of Scarlett O'Hara's
taking over and managing with an iron hand the lumber business of
her husband, romanticized as it may be in the pages of *Gone With
the Wind,* assuredly reflects the true situation of some women of
that period. Hard times had pushed genteel Southerners into positions they were reluctant, even perhaps ashamed, to fill; but on the
positive side, the economic and social conditions of the day provided ironically a certain degree of freedom for women which they
had never experienced before. Eliza accepted Colonel Holbrook's
offer and became the first woman on the *Picayune* staff, indeed one
of the first women in the South to earn her living in such an occupation.

The New Orleans to which Eliza Poitevent moved from her rural
home in Mississippi was a growing metropolis of some two hun-

dred thousand population. Having been captured by Union forces in the early months of the war, the city, like the rest of the South, remained essentially under occupation, suffering from the oppressive Carpetbagger domination. It was a rough and tumble place, in many ways lawless, and the animosity between natives and the outsiders sent South for the ostensible purpose of "reconstructing" the rebellious region fostered an atmosphere in which violence might, and sometimes did, erupt suddenly. The *Picayune,* not surprisingly, supported Democratic candidates and attacked the Republicans who were in power.

In the summer of 1870, the poems of Pearl Rivers began to appear with regularity in the columns of the newspaper, often on the front page, and on 19 February 1871, her first signed article, a narrative of a trip to Pascagoula, Mississippi, was published.[5] In her function as literary editor, she increased the number of poems and book reviews and introduced works of fiction, including stories by nationally famous contemporary authors such as Mark Twain, Joel Chandler Harris, and Bret Harte. "Her constant support of the literary and intellectual life of New Orleans," Lamar Whitlow Bridges writes, "was designed to make New Orleans the 'winter capital of arts and letters,' an ideal she called 'a grand dream.' "[6] Through the columns of her newspaper, she encouraged young writers and endeavored to broaden the literary interests of New Orleaneans in general.

Conscious then as later of the function of a newspaper as an instrument for the dissemination of culture, Eliza Poitevent instituted coverage of art and, in an acknowledgment of the growing female readership, of fashion news. Her editorial decisions, Roger P. McCutcheon states, "were rapid and intuitive rather than cautious, but were usually lucky."[7] This imaginative and serendipitous element in her nature seems to have extended to other areas of her life and to have constituted one of her more endearing traits. Elizabeth Gilmer, a close friend and newspaper associate (best known by her pseudonym Dorothy Dix), was to say of her that she seemed "like little Billee in duMaurier's story, who knew things by the grace of God, without being told."[8] The same precipitous decision-making, one can imagine, must have contributed to her acceptance of Colonel Holbrook's proposal of marriage when he was sixty-four, she only twenty-three. It is conceivable that her family must have objected to the match with as much vehemence as to her having taken a newspaper job, not because of the age difference perhaps —the elderly man with a wife considerably his junior did not constitute an unusual couple in that era—but because Holbrook was divorced. They were, nevertheless, married on 18 May 1872.

One person who decidedly did take exception to the marriage was the first Mrs. Holbrook, who returned to New Orleans from New York shortly after the wedding. On 17 June 1872, she entered the Holbrooks' home on Constance Street and fired twice at Eliza, missing both times. Failing in that effort to remove the woman who had replaced her, she attacked Eliza with a bottle of bay rum and cut her about the head before servants intervened. Afterwards, the first Mrs. Holbrook retrieved an ax from the yard and destroyed a considerable amount of furniture before being subdued by the police and transported to Parish Prison.

Eliza's life with Holbrook, apparently marked by no more such melodramatic incidents, was unfortunately short-lived, for the publisher died only four years after the marriage. The *Picayune*, which Holbrook had sold and repurchased within the space of a year, was found to be in dire financial straits, eighty thousand dollars in debt, facing a two hundred thousand dollar libel suit. Eliza Holbrook, only twenty-seven years old, inexperienced in business matters, a young woman who had grown up in an affluent family, who had been sheltered as a child and young adult, sheltered surely even during her early journalistic career by Holbrook, who must have wanted to protect his protégé and future bride from exposure to the harsh realities of the newspaper world, now had a very serious decision to make, and the options open to her were not promising. She could declare bankruptcy and take the one thousand dollars allowed to a widow under the law, or attempt what must have seemed from her vantage point a well nigh impossible task: she could undertake to save the paper and, in the event that she was able to achieve that difficult goal, then manage that big city daily, something a woman had never before done. Her family urged her to abandon the *Picayune* as a lost cause, to take her widow's allotment, and return to Mississippi. It was at this point, in the centennial year of the United States, that Eliza Poitevent Holbrook called her staff together and informed them of her momentous decision. She would stay and fight; the masthead would be changed to read "Mrs. A. M. Holbrook, Proprietor." How she arrived at her determination, crucial to the history both of the *Picayune* and of women in journalism, one can only guess, but perhaps once again that fortunate intuition was functioning; subsequent events amply justified her daring choice.

"I am a woman," she announced to the motley assemblage of newspapermen at the building on Camp Street that day in 1876. "Some of you may not wish to work for a woman. If so, you are free to go, and no hard feelings. But you who stay—will you give me your undivided loyalty, and will you advise me truly and honestly?"[9] A few of them left—no doubt scared off by the prospect of a lady boss, and a young one at that—but those who remained ("my boys" as she later to referred to them) were indeed fiercely loyal. One, Jose Quintero, even openly proclaimed his willingness to employ his well proven skill as a duelist to defend the paper or its new executive officer should the occasion arise. In later years she was to acknowledge the loyalty of the men around her when she stated that they "work hard to please me, and I verily believe, value a word of commendation from me more than they would the same praise coming from a man."[10] Even with the support of such loyal employees, however, her job was not to be an easy one. She was to recall twenty years later, shortly before her death, the courage required for her decision and the extent of her success: "With me it was sink or swim," she wrote, "and there were not too many friends on the shore trying to throw out life-preservers to save me. I swam out and floated the best I could and have succeeded beyond all expectations."[11]

She was acutely conscious of the advantages of being not merely a woman, but a Southern woman and acknowledged the fact in her interview with Eliza Putnam Heaton in 1887, midway through her remarkable career: "Nowhere except in the South could a woman rule so large an establishment with such ease. I do not say that nowhere else could a woman do it, for nobody knows what a woman can do, least of all the woman herself, until she tries, but only in the South would the difficulties be smoothed away for her, because nowhere else are the men so true and chivalrous." After acknowledging the trepidation with which she undertook her gargantuan task, she asserts that eleven years later she is convinced that with the assistance of "some of my bright young men from the *Picayune*" she could establish a paper in another Southern city.[12] It should be added, however, that in assessing the demands of her position, she wrote in a paper for delivery before the International League of Press Clubs convention in Atlanta, 14 November 1885, "Let me say to any woman who wants to be and can be manager and editor of a great daily newspaper: 'Don't.' "[13]

If Eliza Holbrook's expectations were exceeded, her family members, friends, and foes must have been astounded by the breadth of her accomplishment. The extent of that accomplishment was summed up by Dorothy Dix many years after Eliza's death: "Modern times have developed many good newspaperwomen writers, but Mrs. Nicholson is the only woman who has ever *Made* a big paper."[14] Another contemporary source refers to her in flowery language as "perhaps the only woman in the world who is at the head of a great daily political newspaper, shaping its course, suggesting its enterprises, and actually holding in her slender hands the reins of its government."[15]

Assisting her in the process of transforming the failing newspaper into a major national journal was George Nicholson, an Englishman who became part owner of the business and, on 27 June 1878, the second husband of Eliza Holbrook. If she was, as history would seem to demonstrate, the "newspaper genius" that Thomas Ewing Dabney called her, "with a vision that encompassed new opportunities, and a leadership that opened new trails,"[16] Nicholson's contribution is best summed up in his wife's tribute to his financial acumen:

I believe almost any woman who has brain enough to recognize good newspaper work, and heart enough to appreciate it, could manage the upstairs department of a newspaper, especially if she had such a staff of honorable and competent editors and reporters as I am proud to lean on; but the nerve and brain of a good business man are needed in the down-stairs department of a newspaper, and to Mr. Nicholson more than to any one else do I owe what success I have achieved in journalism.[17]

What specifically constituted that success? What was the remarkable achievement of Eliza Jane Nicholson? In order to understand the magnitude of her twenty years' labor as probably the first woman publisher and editor of a major newspaper in the United States (and even, some sources insist, in the world) it is essential to look at the external and easily measured changes that occurred in the *Picayune* between 1876 and 1896; at the qualities that distinguished Eliza in her life and work; at the specific innovations instituted by the Nicholsons in that period; at the causes to which Eliza devoted her time, energy and money, as well as the support of her newspaper.

The ailing and threatened *Picayune* which she inherited, along with its heavy debts and lawsuits, was an eight-page journal with a circulation of six thousand; but the paper she left as her bequest to her sons twenty years later was a sixteen-page daily (thirty-two pages on Sundays) with a circulation of twenty thousand on weekdays, thirty thousand on Sundays. The paper had grown, however, not only in size but in scope, in content, in purpose. There were now correspondents in such regional spots as Jackson, Mississippi, as well as in Washington, D. C. There were considerably more pictures than before, and other additions included society columns, fashion reports, health advice, articles for children, sports coverage, political cartoons, the Weather Frog (a cartoon-style forecast that remained popular for many years), and news of agriculture and industry. The creation of "the *Picayune* Telephone," a department designed to address readers' complaints about a wide variety of problems from the abuses of businesses to the malfunction of government agencies, foreshadowed the "Action Reporters" of today's television news programs.[18] The physical plant had been expanded with the addition of electric lighting, linotype machines and other printing equipment, as well as telephones which were employed to gain information from other cities in those days before teletype communication.[19]

Ever aware of the changing nature of the paper's readers and their interests, the Nicholsons made a number of innovative additions, some that were patterned after those appearing in other big city dailies, several that were original to the New Orleans publishers. The imagination and daring of Eliza Nicholson is clearly evident in certain of those improvements. She was chiefly responsible for the creation of a woman's page and ever-increasing coverage of matters of interest to women. She gave a new meaning to the phrase "family newspaper" by providing something of interest to readers of both sexes and all ages. Dabney has commented that she observed the growth of the number of female readers and subsequently turned the *Picayune* away from the purely masculine interests of the past. In the process, she created "the newspaper of general interest" and "made the Sunday newspaper the library of the masses."[20] Through the years of her career as publisher and editor, she personally directed the women's section and left her unique stamp upon it. She observed in the *Picayune* in 1879 that although the process was slow in the South, women journalists were "coming to the front"; that the influence of women in all fields was growing; and "that the number of women who read the papers is increasing tremendously."[21]

Innovations, of course, are not always welcome, and one that created a considerable furor in New Orleans—as it perhaps would not have done in any other American city—was the paper's first society column. Not only the Creoles, who were almost pathologically secretive, but also the new rich Americans uptown were, as to some degree their descendants remain even today, jealous of their privacy. (Anyone who doubts it need only consider the exclusive nature of the carnival krewes; for example, the King of Comus, the most prestigious of the organizations, remains anonymous to the general public, despite the tremendous expenses involved in acquiring and filling the role.) Local socialites reacted in emotions ranging from surprise to indignation at the Society Bee, an original presentation of local news notes in the form of a dialogue. As Thomas Ewing Dabney, the newspaper's historian, aptly states it, "no one invaded the privacy of the New Orleans social life until Pearl Rivers loosed the Society Bee on March 16, 1879."[22] Never was there any element of the gossipy in the column, since Eliza was opposed to any sensationalism in her paper. The taboos she established for her staff forbade mention of divorce, sexual scandals, even pregnancies, and prevented the *Picayune*'s giving any significant attention to the problem of prostitution. Dorothy Dix reports a humorous incident in which the editor Nathaniel Burbank, having published a short story about a woman who seduced a young contemporary of her son's, was chastised by Mrs. Nicholson, who informed him "that in the *Picayune* ladies did not seduce their son's friends."[23]

Eliza Nicholson's determination to meet the needs of women readers, combined with her determination to make a place for competent female journalists in her organization, led to the addition of two locally noted and admired columnists, one of whom was ultimately to achieve national fame. Catherine Cole, a friend of the Nicholsons and daughter of W. M. Smallwood, a reporter for the *Picayune*'s financial department, was the columnist whose work most often reflected the opinions of her employer and the causes to which she was devoted. When Eliza Nicholson hired Elizabeth Gilmer, her neighbor at the summer home in Bay St. Louis, she had no way of knowing that she was launching not only one of the most remarkable careers of any woman reporter but also an entirely new, and extremely popular, type newspaper feature; for Gilmer, under her pseudonym Dorothy Dix, was to become the quintessential author of the advice column, and finally to acquire a national reputation not only for answering letters from the lovelorn but also for reporting sensational events for the Hearst syndicate.

Although she could not have been termed a "muckraker" in any sense, given her aversion to sensationalism and exploitation in journalism, there was hardly a worthy cause in New Orleans in the last two decades of the nineteenth century in which Eliza Nicholson was not involved and to which she did not contribute the power of her newspaper. A perusal of Lamar Whitlow Bridges' detailed analysis of the *Picayune* under her aegis reveals paper and publisher speaking out repeatedly on countless public issues: reform in government; the need for a new Louisiana state constitution; the betterment of public education and increase of teachers' wages; improvement in the police force, the fire department, and the electric company; and the purification of water. She directed the newspaper's campaign for prison reform, perhaps under the influence of George Washington Cable. When Louisiana abolished the convict lease system, only the fourth state in the Union to do so, the *Picayune* had played a vital part in the reform. She took a very active role in pioneering reform in the state's asylums, in which mentally ill patients were detained under deplorable conditions.[24]

It was in the area of the protection of animals ("Nature's Dumb Nobility" as she called them) that she most distinguished herself as a philanthropist and activist. From her early years when she wandered in the woods near the Pearl River and became attached to the wild creatures of nature, through her most productive period as a poet when she wrote with a pet canary named Billy Button perched on her finger,[25] to the years of her power as a publisher, she was always concerned with the welfare of dogs and cats, horses and cattle. She campaigned to have watering troughs erected for dray animals in the city; she managed through her editorials and news reports to effect the outlawing of dogfights and bullfights; and she was even capable, a Nicholson family tradition has it, of taking the whip from anyone she observed abusing an animal and lecturing the offender. More importantly, however, she was responsible for establishing in New Orleans a branch of the S.P.C.A., an organization to which she and her paper offered continued support in the form of money and publicity. Both the Nicholsons were several times commended by the American Humane Association for their work in the field, and her efforts achieved for her an international reputation as evidenced by the inclusion of her photograph in a "temple of honor" in Bremen, Germany, dedicated to those who had distinguished themselves in the "sacred cause" of animal welfare.[26]

One finds her devotion to animals not only in her public life but in her private life as well. "Only a Dog," one of her later poems, is the author's answer to some unidentified speaker who has uttered the words of the title upon observing her grief at the death of her dog Mat. The sentiments are those often encountered in poetry dealing with the demise of favorite pets, and perhaps only a true animal lover can respond to it seriously, but the work is prevented

from sinking into the maudlin by the intensity of the anger with
which the speaker counters the condescension toward her grief.

> "Only a dog—a beast," you sneer:
> "Not worthy of a sign or tear."
>   Speak not to me
> Such falsehood of my poor dumb friend
> While I have language to defend
>   His memory.

In the concluding stanza, after having asserted her belief in the
animal's soul, she acknowledges that

> I keep his collar and his bell,
> And do not say to him farewell,
>   But good-bye, Mat,
>   Dear faithful Mat.

The authenticity of Eliza Nicholson's devotion is demonstrated by
the fact that when her personal papers and possessions were recently donated by her descendants to the Historic New Orleans
Collection, Mat's collar was among them.

Eliza Nicholson seems to have shared a view of human beings
attributed to old Ephraim in William Faulkner's *Intruder in the
Dust:* "*If you got something outside the common run that's got to
be done and cant wait, dont waste your time on the menfolks; they
works on . . . the rules and the cases. Get the womens and children
at it; they works on the circumstances.*"[27] In May 1884, she organized the first of several local Bands of Mercy, designed to teach
children to respect and be kind to animals. Out of these groups was
to grow the local S.P.C.A. chapter. When in 1877 problems developed which threatened the completion of a railroad line into the
city, Eliza Nicholson, arguing that women must put "the wheels . . .
in motion," was active in founding the Ladies New Orleans Pacific
Railroad Aid Association and served as secretary of the organization, designed to encourage private subscriptions to complete the
line.[28]

One is amazed to discover the accomplishments of a woman
whose life was relatively short (she died at forty-seven), who reared
a family as well as filling a full-time and demanding position; who
yet managed even in the *Picayune* years to write some poetry,

though much less than before. She was, according to the accounts of those who knew her, surprisingly shy, although with a "nervous and impatient temperament," according to one historian.[29] She was willing always to give her support to worthy organizations and to hold office, but she persistently declined to make public speeches. She was instrumental in founding the Southern Historical Society and the Women's National Press Association, of which she served as president. So extensive did her fame and influence become that she was also elected president of the female journalists' international organization.

Those who have written of her—journalists, historians, cities, and friends—have unanimously agreed on the admirable qualities of the woman and the tremendous scope of her achievement. Dabney asserts that with her talent to inspire rather than merely direct, she gave an "adventurous spirit" back to the *Picayune* and in the process "blazed the trail for women in the changing order."[30] In the *Picayune* on the day following her death, one writer evaluates her career and its impact in glowing terms: "Here was one woman who sought no notoriety, occupied no public place, performed no official function, but in her private capacity as the owner and director of a great newspaper impressed her mind, her character and her individuality on more people than did any other woman in the United States."[31] Dorothy Dix was even less restrained in her praise when she labeled her friend "the only great newspaper woman of the world."[32] Even Bridges, who seems very reticent to praise and certainly careful to put forward all of what he considers Eliza Nicholson's and the *Picayune's* shortcomings—referring to her in a rather amusing understatement, given her unique position, as "something of an innovator in Southern journalism"—admits that she established for herself a national reputation by "rebuilding" the *Picayune* between 1876 and 1896 and, perhaps grudgingly, acknowledges something of her significance in his concluding summary: "Together with her husband, she directed the revival of the newspaper's financial fortunes and the resurgence of the *Daily Picayune* as the leading daily paper in New Orleans."[33]

In the last decade of her life, Eliza was in failing health, suffering from arthritis in her hands and other debilitating ailments; she referred to herself in 1890 as "semi-invalid, chained down to the cushioned ease of a big rocking chair."[34] Despite her condition, the woman who, as Dorothy Dix's biographer remarks, "did not let floods, yellow fever, or other threats bother her,"[35] continued to direct the *Picayune* up to the end of her life. In addition she and her husband, sometimes accompanied by Catherine Cole or other friends, traveled extensively in the United States and in Europe. She was always informed of exactly what was going on in the Camp Street building and, Bridges observes, when important decisions were to be made, "maintained the last word."[36]

In early 1896, both the Nicholsons were stricken with influenza. George died on 4 February, at the age of seventy-six, and Eliza survived her husband by only eleven days. On the morning following her death, the entire front page of the paper she had saved and improved was bordered in black and devoted to her obituary. The Nicholsons are buried in Metairie Cemetery, their tomb marked with a copy of the *Picayune* cast in bronze. Three decades after her death, the Louisiana Iris Society honored her with the Pearl Rivers Rainbow Memorial, an iris-bordered lagoon in City Park.

Catherine Cole, writing of her former employer a week after her death, recalled an occasion on which they had spoken together about eternity. Eliza, taking Catherine's hand, had remarked, "I am not afraid to go, for long since I have had my money's worth."[37] This survey of her life and career, taken with the analysis of her poetry that follows indicates that her life, brief as it was, justified her own evaluation of it.

The career of Eliza Nicholson as newspaper writer, editor, and publisher and her contributions as a philanthropic citizen have been well reported and analyzed by a number of writers. What yet remains to be done, however, is to consider her poetry with critical attention to its strengths and weaknesses, the influences that shaped it, and the patterns of prosody the poet employed. The works to be considered are those included in her one book, *Lyrics*, published by Lippincott in 1873, and one poem subsequently published in a magazine and in pamphlet form. Pearl Rivers was working on a second collection of poems at the time of her death. Unfor-

tunately, much of her verse is to be found only in files of the old
Daily Picayune, other newspapers, and magazines.

Lyrics is a slender green volume stamped in gold, quaintly beautiful in the manner of books of the time, when printing and binding
were still crafts that flourished. The one hundred and thirty-one
pages contain forty-four poems ranging in length from twenty to
one hundred and sixty-four lines, with shorter verses predominat-
ing. The opening poem is entitled "Preface," and its first line,
"God gave a little harp to me," (p. 5) is a concise statement of its
theme and, to judge from her other works dealing with the poet's
art, of the author's philosophy of composition. Talent is a gift of God
and nature, and thus the poet has an obligation as well as a special
place in the universe. In this belief as in numerous other ways, she
is obviously a disciple of the great Romantics, from Wordsworth
and Keats to Emerson and Dickinson, and shares with them common concerns, themes, and technical elements.

Among the most obvious parallels between Pearl Rivers and her
Romantic forebears are her almost Pantheistic devotion to nature as
teacher, speaking a language which the poet is obliged to translate
and impart to ordinary men and women. In "A Whistling Poem,"
she scorns the prim and proper maiden, taught by "prudish Art":

> But I went to school to Nature,
>   And e'er in my class stood high;
> The birds were my merry classmates;
>   They whistle, and why not I? (p. 117)

Elsewhere, expressing an idea that recalls Wordsworth's "The Prelude" and other works, she cites the robin as a pattern of conduct:
"Learn from her my poem lesson,/Nature's teachers are the best"
(p. 48). The persona in "The Singing Heart" describes the process
of a poet's education in typical anti-rationalistic terms:

> An ignorant child—Latin and Greek
>   Were unknown tongues to me;
> But I was quick to catch and speak
>   The tongue of flower and bee. (p. 119)

In "March Month," she again sounds the anti-intellectual note and
seems to echo Wordsworth's "The Tables Turned" when she in-

quires, "What's the use of all this reading?/Not a line is understood.
. . ." Heeding the call of "new sounds in the woods," she turns away
from "grim old Gibbon" who strives to make her wise, for "Fresher
knowledge round me lies." Intuitive knowledge, sent from God, is
to be preferred over that intellectually acquired:

> Now I care more for the building
>   Of the field-lark's humble home,
> Than I do about the raising
>   Of the walls of ancient Rome. (pp. 63–64)

The "impulse from the vernal wood," for Pearl Rivers as for Wordsworth and others who followed him, takes precedence over the
"barren leaves" of books.

Her Pantheistic bent, not so strong as that found in Wordsworth,
is somewhat reminiscent of poems in which Dickinson scoffs
gently at the perfunctory orthodoxy of her family. After acknowledging in "The Singing Heart" that nature was her teacher, Pearl
Rivers moves into the religious sphere with this stanza:

> And when in spring with solemn face
>   Others gave thanks in words,
> For meat and drink, my heart said grace
>   For flowers and for birds. (p. 119)

The result of this reciprocal relationship between nature and the
poet—the one as teacher, guide, divinity (an "all in all" as Wordsworth would have it), and the other as willing student, recipient of
bounty, and worshiper—is that the poet becomes, in a favorite
Romantic metaphor, a translator of "The simple News that Nature
told," a perceptive seer and prophet. Pearl Rivers describes this
sensitivity of the poet:

> My heart has known as little grief
>   As poet's heart can know,
> That quivers like an aspen-leaf
>   At every breath of woe. (p. 130)

So attuned is this special child of nature to the truth, so set apart is
she from the rest of mankind, that as the years pass away, only she,
with her "charmed eye" is able to "track them as they go." (p. 129)
Such passages amply indicate the debt of Pearl Rivers to the Ro-

mantic poets and suggest that the impulses which inspired her
were similar to those that inspired her illustrious predecessors.

A majority of the poems in *Lyrics* are composed in four-line
stanzas, but within those confines she employs a considerable variety of rhythmical patterns. There is the traditional ballad stanza of
"Preface," for example:

> Sometimes my songs are low and sad,
>   And thrill with tender woe;
> Sometimes my songs are light and glad,
>   Because my heart is so. (p. 5)

In "Midsummer" she employs four four-beat lines, a favorite form,
with a basic iambic beat. Consider, for example, this stanza, distinguished by its hint of sensuality, rare for her early poetry:

> With parted lips and half-shut eyes,
>   Like some fair maiden in a swoon,
> O'ercome with heat the morning lies
>   Breathless across the lap of noon. (p. 31)

Another frequently employed form is the trochaic tetrameter line,
exemplified by this stanza from "March Freaks":

> Ah! the early roses know me,
>   Forth they stretch their tender palms;
> I must read their happy fortunes
>   And receive their fragrant alms. (p. 65)

Occasionally she experiments with a mixture of metrical feet as in
"Reveille":

> Unlock all your pearly gates,
>   With diamond keys, oh, dew!
> By the golden light of the stars to-night
>   Let the souls of the flowers through. (p. 18)

Other poems are built of five-line or eight-line stanzas with varying
numbers and kinds of feet. Whatever the form, the degree of skill
displayed in handling it suggests that Pearl Rivers, if "innocent of
prosody," was certainly gifted with a musical ear and a talent for
beneficial imitation.

Her similes, metaphors, and other figures of speech are often, as
might be expected, drawn from nature. Some are simple—the poet

as bird, her skill as a harp, the new year as a babe—but in several poems she prolongs a metaphor into a conceit, even into an allegory. In one work, the comparison between the physical, mental and spiritual elements of the persona and a factory is drawn out into an elaborate, almost metaphysical, conceit, somewhat reminiscent of Poe. In the center of the factory the "Heartwheel," turned by Love, moves all the other wheels, including Hope, Joy, and Duty. In its "high and spacious chamber," the "Brain-wheel," turned by Thought, weaves "threads of every hue." The god who "upreared this noble structure" has an Age of Reason quality about him; after setting "the wheels in motion," he charged the persona to keep them "bright and busy." The factory is besieged by such personifications as Care, Sloth, Mother Gossip, Pleasure, and Envy, but they are driven away by the watchmen, Faith and Prayer (pp. 36–39). In "The Three Physicians," the speaker, sick of soul with "a cross that I bore in secret" and a "grief that I could not forget," seeks counsel from Dr. Mirth ("the World's Physician") and from Dr. Travel ("the rich man's Physician"); finally, their cures having failed, the speaker turns to Dr. Patience, son of "old Mother Religion" and brother of "Sister Mercy," and is restored to health (pp. 52–54).

The language of Pearl Rivers' poetry is uncomplicated, even in such an ornate work as the allegories cited above. The straightforward statement is not surprising in the young poet, of course; and in the later work, her newspaper training, despite the fact that journalists were more flowery in those days than in Hemingway's time, would perhaps have encouraged the economical and simple words that distinguish her work. There are few characters in the poems, except of the generic type, and few dramatic incidents, except those of nature's world. The tone is often mystical, usually idealistic, only occasionally ironic or sarcastic or bitter. The god who rules over the world of her verse is variously a deistic watchmaker, as in the allegory above, or the kindly father; but interestingly, given the time of composition, there is no mention, in the poetry of *Lyrics* or in the four works later published in pamphlets, of Christ, the Crucifixion, or other elements of Christian orthodoxy.

The range of subject matter found in the poems of *Lyrics* is not wide; like Dickinson, Pearl Rivers seemed content to mine a narrow vein of ore, but mine it well. Most often she writes of nature, of all the seasons, but particularly of Spring and Summer, more particularly of the months of March, April, May. A number of works are devoted to poets and the art of poetry, these too linked to nature, which is credited along with God for the gift of creativity. Several verses comment on the passage of time, and several glorify the virtues of patience and the acceptance of one's lot. Another favorite virtue, the subject of a number of works and an element in many others, is simplicity. One special group of poems are those constructed around the sorrows of a woman's heart and the pains of unrequited love.

The themes that Pearl Rivers develops from the subjects to which she turned her attention are essentially those one would expect from a disciple of the Romantics living in mid-nineteenth century America. The range of themes is limited, and most of them are in some way developments of a consideration of the relationship between human beings and nature, with an omnipotent but benevolent god hovering in the background as a kind of divine stage manager of the action in this basic drama. The nature poems possess always a delicacy that no doubt contributed to making them popular in their day. (One contemporary critic described them as being "so dainty they might have been etched with a thorn on the petal of a dog-rose bloom.")[38]

The qualities of nature which Pearl Rivers celebrates are its beauty, majesty, and simple perfection; and these, she argues, are God-given for the purpose of guiding, consoling and shaping man if he is willing to accept the bounty offered him. In March, one of the poet's favorite months, "Budding Beauty" is described as running, "bold and naked," finally to "clothe herself in April" and "grow shy and blush in May" (p. 63). The external world which she presents in verse after verse is one that is simple, yet portrayed in language symbolic of great wealth, as in "The Court":

> In the Golden Land of Sunshine,
>   Near the Silvery Land of Dew,
> Where the air is pure and fragrant
>   And the skies are always blue. . . . (p. 74)

And in this realm dwell the royalty of nature, lords and ladies of the seasons. The poet states, for example, that:

> Not within a lordly castle,
>   But beneath a tent of green,
> In a golden robe of glory,
>   Stood fair May, the reigning Queen. (p. 74)

May, alternately a lady and a Queen, along with March and April, recur in a number of poems in a majestic setting, and when Spring comes, it is in a "Royal Cavalcade":

> From the busy Court of Nature
>   Rides the fair young Queen in state,
> O'er the road of perfect Weather,
>   Leading down to Summer Gate. (p. 9)

In "The Royal Funeral," spring, "the Virgin Queen," is dead, replaced by "a young voluptuous sister," and will lie in state until the "Sad pallbearers of the dead" come to bury her in "the distant Autumn Country" (p. 14). The poem immediately following, not surprisingly, is "Reveille," in which an apostrophe to the locust instructs him to sound his "magical hidden drum" to announce the coming of the new spring.

> All the earth is so fresh and green,
>   And life such a pleasant thing,
> Oh the Lord I bless, and in joy possess
>   My portion in his new spring. (pp. 17–18)

Despite the royal trappings of the spring poems, it is the simplicity of nature that the poet most admires. The ability of the simple animal, human being, or virtue to encounter and overcome pride and vanity, again through the agency of a benevolent and all-seeing God, is a favorite unifying element in her poems. What ultimately inspires her most is not the grand dramatic activities in nature, but the quiet dawn, the subtle twilight; not the exotic animal, but the spider, the sparrow, the locust, the honeybee; not the bright and splashy plant life, but the daisy, the violet, the withered cornstalk. These are simple and, as the persona persists in telling us, so is she, an uncomplicated singer with an uncomplex song. Like Dickinson and Thoreau before her, she obviously feels it is in that simplicity that one finds the beauty, joy and power of the song.

One distinctive aspect of the simple nature of creatures as portrayed by Pearl Rivers is the willingness to accept one's position in life, however low or seemingly unimportant it may be. In "A Chirp From Mother Robin," the "character" of the title, despite the fact that "Other nests are lined more softly," is contented with her lot. Her nest, she says, is large enough and warm enough for her brood. Although her cousin "Madame Red" is more grandly arrayed, she accepts her own "robe of graver colors," "For the Master knew what costume/Would become a robin best" (pp. 48–49). The speaker in "What The Sparrow Chirps," like the robin, recognizes his low estate and welcomes it as part of the divine plan, consoled by the fact that "our Heavenly Father" knows whenever "one of us falls to the ground" (p. 51). The same patient acceptance in the human realm is the subject of "Poor and Proud," in which an impoverished mother, scorned by a wealthy woman, explains the basis of her own pride. The rich woman, who sold herself for gold, is barren, while the poor woman is rich in the love of her husband and child. Again, simplicity triumphs over position and power and gold.

In "The Contrast," the two elements of the natural world, royalty and simplicity, are portrayed in a dramatic counterpoint. The "Daisy poor," first speaker in the poem, inquires of the "great rich Sunflower" why he has come "a-wooing" at her humble door. She admonishes him to

> Go to the court of Nature,
>   And win you a stately bride,
> With beauty, and wealth, and station,
>   To match with your birth and pride.

He should consider Lady Tulip or Princess Lily, argues the Daisy, for she herself is "only a peasant," who would be the object of scorn for the ladies of the court. The Sunflower assures her that it is not for beauty, wealth, birth or station that he pays her court, but because of her "modest worth."

> So men of the Sunflower spirit,
> > Seeking the wide world through,
> Mate with the Daisy women—.
> > Simple, and sweet, and true. (p. 60)

The sentiment seems almost contradictory to what one might expect from a woman whose life and career would seem not quite that of the simple "Daisy women" described in the concluding stanza; but in nature, poetry and life, if we are to judge from her own compositions, Eliza Nicholson—at least in the guise of Pearl Rivers—put a high premium on simplicity.

Poetry she sees as the bounty of God to the chosen few, a theme first voiced in the Preface. The Singer, with her God-given "little harp," will sing, not like David or the great English bards of the Middle Ages, but to the best of her abilities. When she dies, her harp, she predicts, will not be hung in "the echoing halls of Fame" with those of great master singers, but rather passed on to lovers "of the simple thing," "Because of simple joys and woes/The Singer used to sing" (pp. 5–6). In "The Rainbow," the poet speaks not only of the arc of colors in the sky but also of the one God placed in her heart when she was a child, a bow made of "smiles and tears," which grew, as body and heart matured, to become

> A wider bow, a fairer bow,
> And tenderer than the one
> That is a bright betrothal pledge
> Between the rain and sun.

Now, the inner rainbow grows larger, shines brighter, the more the speaker sympathizes with "human joy and woe,"

> For sunny smiles and dewy tears
> Must always blended be
> In every heart in which God sets
> The rainbow Poesie. (pp. 25–27)

The divine gift of creativity becomes for the recipient not merely a blessing but also an obligation, for she is required to sympathize with the joy and pain of mankind. Like John Keats, Pearl Rivers seems convinced here, as in several other poems, that life is a blend of the bitter and the sweet.

"The Singing Heart" is another poem in which the poet attributes to God the gifts of her creative power, a closeness to nature, and an awareness of its beauty and goodness. The world has "bruised" the poet and Slander has pierced her "with a poisoned dart,"

> But singing hearts are hard to kill,
> And God made mine with wings,
> To fly above all earthly ill;
> And so it lives and sings. (pp. 119–21)

In her "Whistling Poem," probably the most often quoted by her biographers, Pearl Rivers presents much the same view of the pain that the poet must face and the therapeutic value of song when she observes that "Life is a rugged country/And whistling helps uphill" (p. 117). The singer-whistler-poet, then, has a definite purpose in God's creation: to sympathize with man in his pleasure and pain and to ease his way through what Keats called "the vale of Soul-making."

One final recurrent theme is that associated with the heart of a woman suffering the pangs of unrequited love or rejection. The skillful lyric "Under the Snow" presents a woman, spurned by the man she loves, who tears love out of her heart, crushes it in her hand, and, having "shrouded it with your cold cold words," buries it under the snow.

> Then with my murderous hands
> I raised up the heavy stone
> Of *Silence* over my buried love,
> Lest the world should hear it moan. (p. 21)

It is a strangely moving poem, expressing strong and even violent emotions in sharp contrast to the gentle sentiments of her nature poetry. A similar bitterness pervades "Only a Heart," in which another woman scorned addresses the man who has rejected her in language heavily ironic. It is, she tells him, only a heart, not a stone, serpent, thorn, or sword to injure his foot:

> Only a heart, a woman's heart,
> Step on it! crush it! so!
> Bravely done like a gentleman,
> Turn on your heel and go.

He need not trouble himself, the persona continues, with any pain he may have caused it, for "Such hearts are as plenty as summer leaves." In the concluding stanza, the emotions are diametrically opposed to those of her lyrics which praise patience, simplicity, and the benevolence of an all knowing Heavenly Father:

> Only a heart! do not fear, my lord,
>   Nobody on earth is near
> To come to the cry of the wounded thing,
>   And God is too far to hear.

The divinity in the last line is akin to the god of the Deists, powerful but withdrawn, unaffected by individual suffering, and the irony is almost that of Hardy. The same topic and the same emotions were to be repeated in her most powerful work, published twenty years after the appearance of *Lyrics*.

It is in many ways regrettable that there was no second volume of poetry from Pearl Rivers, since there is evidence of considerable growth in the works included in *Lyrics*. Such a poem as "Hagar," published in *Cosmopolitan* in 1893, suggests that the poet was ready to embark on a new kind of writing, with a new style and a favorite subject from the past handled in a startlingly different way.

The reading of the poet had obviously included by the time of the composition of "Hagar" the poems of Robert Browning. Such an early work as "Only a Heart" seems to echo in its closing line, quoted above, the ending of "Porphyria's Lover," but by 1893, Pearl Rivers had adopted the dramatic monologue, a much more sophisticated form than her earlier lyrics, and had given it her distinctive stamp to produce a powerful evocation of the woman scorned. Not surprisingly, the poem seems not to have received much understanding or appreciation from the critics of her time. Roger P. McCutcheon observed in his sketch of Pearl Rivers for the *Dictionary of American Biography* that "Hagar" and "Leah," a similar but less effective dramatic monologue published the year after the first, are "ambitious," but "in spite of good lines," they are "rhetorical rather than passionate." Although her emotions are evidently sincere, he concludes, they are "sometimes obscured by inadequate technique and expression."[39] Even James Henry Harrison, in his generally sensitive 1932 study of her life and work, passes over "Hagar" and "Leah," saying of them only that they are "built around Biblical themes."[40] No critic, finally, seems to have done justice to what is undoubtedly the best of Pearl Rivers' poems, as well as an early document of feminist literature, and, most importantly, a work worthy of inclusion in any anthology of American poetry.

"Hagar" is composed of one hundred and sixty lines of unrhymed iambic pentameter. Pearl Rivers' control of blank verse is sure, unfaltering, and despite the regular beat of the lines, there is a conversational quality to them worthy of Browning. The poet has taken the briefly recounted story of the Egyptian bondswoman from the book of Genesis and elaborated characters and incidents into an intense and credible drama. In the Biblical version, Hagar has borne a son, Ishmael, to Abraham; when Sara, Abraham's wife, also gives birth to a son, Isaac, she urges her husband to drive Hagar away, and at God's command, he does so, having provided his mistress and child with water and bread for their desert journey.

Pearl Rivers wisely chooses to begin her poem at a very crucial point in the action: Abraham, after issuing his edict, has come to Hagar's tent, where she greets him with her exclamation, those startling opening words of the poem, "Go back!" Surely the most essential element of a good dramatic monologue is a strong, believable character, one who through his or her words reveals more than the words intend. Hagar is yet another of the poet's scorned women, a character to whom no previous writer had ever given much thought apparently; like the persona in "A Woman's Heart," she is fiercely angry, bitter, and surprisingly strong. The entirety of this monologue is spoken to Abraham, and the opening lines, designed to command the reader's attention and hold it, set the tone for the rest:

> Go back! How dare you follow me beyond
> The door of my poor tent? Are you afraid
> That I have stolen something? See, my hands
> Are empty, like my heart. I am no thief![41]

The image of the woman's heart is to reappear throughout the poem as an indication of the degree of suffering to which Hagar has been subjected. She assures Abraham that the gifts he has given her in the past she has thrown away, scorning to take with her anything that would remind her of the man she refers to ironically as "my generous lord."

By this point, the author has so skillfully manipulated the reader's feelings that his sympathy is with Hagar; and Sara, in a reversal of the Biblical situation, becomes the villain. See where she stands, Hagar says,

> Watching us there, behind the flowering date,
> With jealous eyes, lest my poor hand should steal
> One farewell touch from yours.

Go back and tell her, Hagar commands, that her heart, proud as Sara's, may break, but it will be without tears, "like iron; hard but clean," asking no pity. The growing violence of her emotions is graphically represented by the image the poet employs to convey her contempt:

> If my lips
> Should let one plea for mercy slip between
> These words that lash you with a woman's scorn,
> My teeth should bite them off, and I would spit
> Them at you, laughing, though all red and warm
> with blood.

She further threatens to pluck out her eyes if they should weep, to have her son cut off her hands should they touch Abraham's and cling to them "against my will." The word "will" here is significant, for the entire work concerns itself largely with the struggle between a woman's will and her wounded heart, betrayed but still in love.

Hagar proceeds to question Sara's love for Abraham and to describe the intensity of her own, so strong, she says, that at his touch or voice her heart was overwhelmed. In a tone rather more erotic than was usual for poetry in the 1890s, especially that by a woman and with a Biblical theme, Hagar asserts that Abraham's flesh is so dear to her that

> There is no vein
> That branches from your heart, whose azure course
> I have not followed with my kissing lips.

She would, she declares, have died to save him any time. When he was ill she lay outside his tent without food or drink until he was well again. The poet's love of animals is exemplified by the introduction of Abraham's horse, Benammi, whose neck Hagar had thrown her arms around in her sorrow over his master's illness.

> Your good horse understood,
> And gently rubbed his face against my head,
> To comfort me.

Abraham, in contrast, spoke no words of comfort to her, giving all of his tenderness instead to Sara.

Now he sends her forth into the wilderness, not well provisioned nor riding a camel, "as my mistress rides," but on foot with only "A jug of water, and—a loaf of bread—" for sustenance. The depth and changeability of Hagar's emotions are subtly suggested by the poet's use of dashes, which indicate, as the words that follow make clear, a break in the speaker's voice. But "That sound was not a sob," she defensively insists; "I only lost/ My breath and caught it hard again." She repeats then the words that have become the poem's refrain: "Go back!"

In the next section Hagar questions the mercy of a god who would command that she be driven out, her heart broken. Weakening in her resolve to remain aloof, to scorn him and his wife, she begs Abraham to flee with her to Egypt, leaving the wealth to Sara:

> Sara loves
> The touch of costly linen and the scent
> Of precious Chaldean spices, and to bind
> Her brow with golden fillets, and perfume
> Her hair with ointment. Sara loves the sound
> Of many cattle lowing on the hills;
> And Sara loves the slow and stealthy tread
> Of many cattle moving on the plains.
> Hagar loves you.

The contrast—the catalog of Sara's devotion to the material juxtaposed to the brief message of the last three words—is an effective touch, again reminiscent of passages in Browning's monologues.

Observing a frown on Abraham's face, Hagar abruptly turns again to the bitterness of her rejection, denying that it was her voice that spoke such pleading words. "Go back!" she shouts at him again,

> And tell your God I hate him, and I hate
> The cruel craven heart that worships him
> And dare not disobey.

Accusing Abraham of cowardice and fear of his wife, Hagar prepares to go, proud, she asserts, that she takes none of his riches with
her and would indeed spurn even the water and the bread "If it
were not for Ishmael's dear sake." Her son will become a desert
prince, she vows, echoing the prophecy in Genesis, "Whose hands
shall be against all other men." Uttering a curse that for Abraham
all bread shall henceforth "taste bitter with my hate," the sweetest
water "salty with my tears," she swears by Egypt's gods that she
will surely be avenged. With an ironic "Farewell," she fiercely
prophesies that

> . . . the wrongs that you have done this day
> Shall waken and uncoil themselves, and hiss
> Like adders at the name of Abraham.

On that note of ferocious anger, expressed in words chosen and
arranged to reflect meaning and emotion, the poem ends.

When one takes into consideration the time and place and culture
in which "Hagar" was composed, it seems a stunning achievement,
far in advance of its time. Though some of the early lyrics of the
poet are somewhat quaint by today's standards, decidedly of an age
long past, this dramatic monologue could have been written yester-
day. Among its virtues are a clarity of language not always easily
accomplished in the framework of verse; a remarkably subtle control of emotions that reflects the poet's understanding of human
psychology, particularly as regards the woman scorned; and, growing out of that understanding, a memorable and fascinating character who is, despite the almost murderous intensity of her anger,
credible and, most amazing of all, sympathetic. Such a work of art, it
must be said again, can only make the appreciative reader grieve
that the quantity of the poet's work was limited.

One of the works in *Lyrics* in which the author defended her own
distinctive way of writing contains the statement, "Nature made the
poet daring,/I will sing my own wild way" (p. 85). With "Hagar,"
those early words acquire a new meaning. The paradox of the wild

emotions in "Hagar," held in check by the controlling consciousness of the poet, indicates the real extent of the daring of the writer
who called herself Pearl Rivers.

NOTES

[1]*Biographical and Historical Memoirs of Louisiana* (Chicago: Goodspeed, 1892),
II, 277.

[2]Pearl Rivers, *Lyrics* (Philadelphia: Lippincott, 1873), p. 119. All further references to this work appear in the text.

[3]Thomas Ewing Dabney, *One Hundred Great Years: The Story of the Times-
Picayune from Its Founding to 1940* (Baton Rouge: Louisiana State Univ. Press,
1944), p. 261.

[4]Dabney, p. 261.

[5]James Henry Harrison, *Pearl Rivers: Publisher of the Picayune* (New Orleans:
Tulane Univ. 1932), p. 7; Dabney, p. 261.

[6]Lamar Whitlow Bridges, "A Study of the New Orleans *Daily Picayune* Under
Publisher Eliza Jane Poitevent Nicholson, 1876–1896," Diss. Southern Illinois
Univ. 1974, p. 160. Bridges' dissertation is a valuable source for information on the
Picayune during Mrs. Nicholson's career as publisher. Much of the factual informa-
tion on that aspect of her life employed in this paper is drawn from his work.

[7]Roger P. McCutcheon, *Dictionary of American Biography* (New York: Charles
Scribner's Sons, 1934), XIII, 499.

[8]Dorothy Dix, *Times-Picayune*, 25 Jan. 1937, Sec. E, p. 4.

[9]Dabney, p. 266.

[10]Interview with Eliza Putnam Heaton, 8 Oct. 1887, quoted in Dabney, p. 305.

[11]Quoted in *Times-Picayune*, 21 April 1932.

[12]Interview with Eliza Putnam Heaton, 8 Oct. 1887, quoted in Harrison, p. 22.

[13]Harrison, p. 26.

[14]Quoted by Elsie S. Farr, "Pearl Rivers," *Times-Picayune*, 11 March 1951, Dixie-
Roto Section, p. 7.

[15]*Biographical and Historical Memoirs of Louisiana*, II, 277.

[16]Dabney, p. 304.

[17]*The National Cyclopedia of American Biography* (Ann Arbor: University Micro-
films, 1964), I, 309.

[18]Harrison, p. 57.

[19]Bridges, passim.

[20]Dabney, pp. 307, 309.

[21]From *Daily Picayune*, 30 March 1879, quoted in Bridges, p. 233. In view of this
quotation, Bridges' evaluation of Eliza Nicholson as "not a 'feminist'" (p. 230) seems
odd.

[22]Dabney, p. 307.

[23]Bridges, pp. 112–113; Harnett Kane and Ella Bentley Arthur, *Dear Dorothy Dix*
(Garden City: Doubleday, 1952), p. 57.

[24]Bridges and Dabney, passim.

[25]Bridges, p. 11.

[26]Harrison, p. 51.

[27]William Faulkner, *Intruder in the Dust* (New York: Random House, 1948), p.
112.

[28]Bridges, pp. 62–63.

[29]Harrison, p. 63.

[30]Dabney, pp. 304–305; Dabney, The *Times-Picayune*, 25 Jan. 1937, Sec. A, p. 2.

[31]Harrison, p. 29.

[32]Dorothy Dix, quoted in "Dedication of Memorial for Pearl Rivers," *Times-Picayune*, 21 April 1932.

[33]Bridges, pp. 230, 306, 317.

[34]Quoted in Bridges, p. 287.

[35]Kane, p. 55.

[36]Bridges, p. 287.

[37]Quoted by Catherine Cole, *Daily Picayune*, 23 February 1896.

[38]*Biographical and Historical Memoirs of Louisiana*, II, 277.

[39]McCutcheon, XIII, 499.

[40]Harrison, p. 28.

[41]"Hagar," in *An Anthology of Mississippi Writers* (Jackson: Univ. Press of Mississippi, 1979), pp. 134–39. Subsequent quotations are from this source.

Christianity and Catholicism in the Fiction of Kate Chopin

THOMAS BONNER, JR.

Kate Chopin grew up in an institutionally and culturally religious environment. The greater part of her life in Louisiana and St. Louis was spent in areas of the country where the culture was uniquely Roman Catholic: her schooling in St. Louis under the Sisters of the Sacred Heart, a French order; her early years of marriage in New Orleans under the influences of the American Cathedral, St. Patrick's, and the French one, St. Louis; the years near Natchitoches, a French Catholic community, and her later years back in St. Louis, a city-scape dominated by church steeples.

Despite the orthodox milieu in which Chopin was reared, she came to possess an independent and inquiring spirit. Biographical evidence, most recently revealed by Per Seyersted, shows her to have been indifferent to the obligation of the Sabbath while she was in Europe on her wedding trip. Her taking solitary walks and drinking in the beer halls also suggests a slight impertinence to tradition.[1] Furthermore, much of her fiction explores a dark side of human nature, largely untouched by male or female writers in the nineteenth century. The most exquisite example of this trait can be found in her novel *The Awakening*, in which a young matron leaves her husband, nearly rejects her children, and engages in sexual activity with someone whom she does not love.

And yet the landscapes of Chopin's narratives reveal the vestiges of her ecclesiastical experience. She composed her fiction on a solidly realistic base, and the elements of Catholicism provide a distinguishing texture. While the theme of Christian love extends throughout the stories, Chopin also developed themes criticizing ecclesiastical customs and practices. Furthermore, feast days, rituals, and icons often serve as devices contributing to the fictive structures. A study of Chopin's uses of Christianity and Catholicism

118

reflects a running tension between obligations to the self and to the community, a major concern in her novels and short stories.

The theme of Christian love, emanating from the second great commandment to love one's neighbor as oneself, requires a de-emphasis of the self in favor of another. The heroic response to the law results in selflessness. "Marse Chouchoute," "Ma'ame Péla-gie," "A Dresden Lady in Dixie," "Ozème's Holiday," and "Tante Cat'rinette" emphasize Chopin's interest in this noble idea.

Wash, a white boy, undertakes a responsibility to deliver the community mail to the train station in "Marse Chouchoute." One evening he is delayed at a social gathering, and his black friend realizes that he will lose his job if the mail is not delivered. In the night he takes the mail horse and races for the depot; in the haste to meet the train the horse stumbles, and the youngster falls between wheels and rails to his death. Much of the narrative focuses on the black youngster's concern that Wash's failure to meet his responsi-bilities will have a devastating effect on his life and family. He does not reflect on the danger in which his mission places him, and it appears that his measurement of happiness is directly proportion-ate and identifiable with that of his white friend.

In "Ma'ame Pélagie," a story set not long after the close of the Civil War, an older sister, in order to secure happiness for her younger sibling with whom she had been living for a number of years, gives up her dream of restoring their war-ravaged home so that the youth could enter the community of the post-war era. A small house is built, and social intercourse with the river communi-ties begins anew. Unlike the hero of the previous story, Ma'me Pélagie feels the sacrifice keenly: "While the outward pressure of a young and joyous existence had forced her footsteps into the light, her soul had stayed in the shadow of the ruin."[2] Similarly, in "Tante Cat'rinette" a black woman offers to give up her independ-ence and property for the daughter of her old mistress in order to preserve the well-being of her family. Cat'rinette like Ma'me Péla-gie struggles toward a decision and makes it in light of an epiphany received in the hours before dawn along a road: "And steeped in the splendor of [that morning sky] hung one pale star; there was not another in the whole heaven . . . her eyes fixed intently upon that star, which held her like a hypnotic spell" (I, 343).

When Pa-Jeff, the old black man of "A Dresden Lady in Dixie," gives up his honor to protect the innocence of Agapie, a daughter of the mistress of the house, he assumes heroic proportions. Despite great internal turbulence—a "real" or imagined battle between the spirit and the devil—the old man takes the blame for a missing piece of china. As a result the girl is cleared of suspicion and accepted once again into her society. Because another person knows her soul, she must work to redeem herself, the dark reminder nearly always in sight. The story borders on the sentimental but its humor keeps it from transgressing.

Chopin's characters often perform acts of kindness across racial barriers; these are on occasion accompanied by a certain discomfort. The white protagonist of "Ozème's Holiday" gives up his vacation to aid a black woman who had at one time helped him. He performs field, kitchen, and nursing tasks for the ailing woman. When Ozème returns to his regular work, he is unable to admit to his fellow workers that he really had no vacation. From one aspect the conflict centers on Ozème's inability to reconcile his act of charity with the values of his companions, who simply would not understand a white person's sacrifice for a black person.

Chopin's stories in pursuit of the theme of Christian love go beyond mere exemplar. The characters and the dialogue are indeed vital, and one finds a tension between their functions that delights and informs. However, she was also working toward a more complex treatment of a major spiritual theme, involving in part the strictures of Roman Catholicism and their infringement on the individual's freedom of choice. Her first novel *At Fault* gives a considerable hint by intimating that there is a higher value than the love of one person for another. In denying Thérèse and Hosmer the opportunity of marriage at the outset, Chopin has Thérèse emphasize that "love isn't everything in life; there is something higher" (II, 769). Although she implies an order of responsibility extending beyond the self, Thérèse states that moral principle is "peculiarly one's own" (II, 766), and she intimates that one does not force her will on others.

Thérèse then exacts her will on Hosmer, this act providing the basis of the conflict; the major contributing element despite her

protests is Thérèse's embrace of the Roman Catholic law pro-
hibiting divorce and remarriage by a divorced person. Thérèse,
a young widow and chatelaine of a plantation, grows to love Hosmer, a lumber mill manager from St. Louis. When she realizes that
he has divorced his wife, she convinces him that he should return
to remarry her as an act of higher responsibility. When this plan
fails, Thérèse still will not marry him despite her great affection
for him. As this novel was Chopin's first, her failure to reconcile the
dilemma through the forces of the characters is understandable.
Instead, she sails around canon law by having Hosmer's wife
drown in a river accident; thus the impediment to marriage is
removed.

Nearly ten years later when Chopin was writing *The Awakening,*
she was still wrestling with the problem of a Church-sanctioned
marriage and the ramifications of its dissolution. Chopin's concern
about "not forcing one's will on another" emerges in this work.
Edna Pontellier, a twenty-eight year old matron, decides to withdraw from the obligations of her marriage to Léonce Pontellier in
order to pursue her own life. However, her husband and her friend
Madame Ratignolle naturally exert pressure on her to accept her
traditional domestic role. Rejecting their appeals, Edna moves in
stages from her bonds, finally leaving residence in the family home
for a nearby cottage.

Chopin does not take on the problem of divorce in this novel. She
must have realized that if divorce were considered as an alternative
for Edna, the censure which was sure to come would be so complete as to create a living death for the heroine. She also fortunately
avoids the *deus ex machina* device which resolved the conflict in
At Fault. By choosing suicide for Edna, Chopin creates a more
critically correct solution for her protagonist's dilemma, for the
elements which contribute to her decision rise from her own
psyche and the forces of her peculiar circumstances. Edna does not
allow another's will to be forced upon her, but she visits disaster
upon herself as the final solution.

The Catholic presence in both novels goes beyond the canonical
nature of the themes, for Chopin satirizes the religious practices of
Catholicism in showing the practitioners are in fact hollow shells of

faith. In *At Fault* she describes Belle Worthington: "This lady was a good Catholic to the necessary extent of hearing a mass on Sundays, abstaining from meat on Fridays and Ember Days, and making her 'Easters.' Which concessions were not without their attendant discomforts, counterbalanced, however, by the soothing assurance which they gave her of keeping on the safe side" (II, 784). Chopin lets Mr. Worthington, who apparently does not accompany his wife to church, speak pompously on the value of religion: "As you would find, my dear sir, by following carefully the history of mankind, that the religious sentiment is implanted, a true and legitimate attribute of the human soul—with peremptory right to its existence. Whatever may be faulty in the creeds—that makes no difference, the foundation is there and not to be dislodged" (II, 792). This blast of the trumpet was brought on by his visitor's statement that "all religions are but mythical creations invented to satisfy a species of sentimentality—a morbid craving in man for the unknown and undemonstrable" (II, 792). In another scene the riotous Grégoire receives a personal sermon on hell from Père Antoine, to which he responds by arguing against the existence of hell, leaving his presence, and firing his pistol. He dies shortly afterwards as a result of his inclination to violence. Père Antoine's activities are described by a black servant, who gives the priest a near minstrel-like image.

In *The Awakening* Chopin continues to address the legalisms and excessive pieties which fly in the face of a real faith. The lady in black who invariably follows the young lovers about on Grand Isle is the principal vehicle in this pursuit. Chopin creates her as a functional single-faceted character; one neither sees her face nor hears her. She is simply there, perhaps as a dark reminder of an outworn custom or as a symbol for empty practices. Two passages offer the range of her role. The first touches on the excesses of ornament in relation to function: "The lady in black, with her Sunday prayer-book, velvet and gold-clasped, and her Sunday silver beads was following them at no great distance" (II, 913). The second touches on the old subject of indulgences and their accrued legalisms: "The lady in black had once received a pair of prayer-beads of curious workmanship from Mexico, with very special indulgence attached to them, but she had never been able to ascertain whether the indulgence extended outside the Mexican border. Father Fochel of the Cathedral had attempted to explain it; but he had not done so to her satisfaction. And she begged that Robert [who was going to Mexico] would interest himself, and discover, if possible, whether she was entitled to the indulgence accompanying the remarkably curious Mexican prayer-beads" (II, 923–24). The lightly humorous tone has a precedent in "Madame Célestin's Divorce," in which the wife appears to consult the entire hierarchy from her confessor to the Pope on the matter of divorce. Chopin does not exhibit rancor on these aspects of religion and its practice, but she is aggressive in reaching for the truth despite the sensitivity of subject.

Chopin's uses of rituals, clergy, feast days, and other related references are not limited in their applications. In *The Awakening* the emphasis on the mystical nature of the Gulf of Mexico at Grand Isle finds reinforcement in the name of the island church—Our Lady of Lourdes, which recalls the small community in France known for the miraculous cures which the blessed waters have allegedly effected. Edna Pontellier's awakenings of soul, intellect, and senses become one with her experiences in the warm water of the Gulf: first her being afraid of the water, then her enjoying its sensuous grasp, and finally her finding it comfortable enough for death. In the short fiction especially, Chopin employs these religious elements as both thematic and structural devices.

The holy days of Easter and Christmas figure in the development of seven stories. In "A Morning Walk" Chopin uses the spirit of renewal associated with the Easter season to underscore the awakening of a poetic vision. At the services the minister intones, "I am the Resurrection and the Life," and in Archie's soul "a vision of life came with it; the poet's vision, of the life that is within and the life that is without, pulsing in unison, breathing the harmony of an undivided existence" (II, 569). In "Love on the Bon-Dieu," travel to the local church for confession to prepare for Easter composes the basic device for the narrative structure. Two young people meet, see each other on consecutive Sundays, miss each other one day, and after a brief search seal their marital intentions.

All the events are coordinated so that the church is always central in the lives of the characters. Monsieur Michel, a hermit in "After the Winter," is reunited to his community when, at first enraged at children picking his flowers for Easter, he follows them to the village to complain but there rediscovers his friends who are chanting the *Gloria* at the church. He is moved to the beginnings of change by the refrain *"Gloria in excelsis"*: "Where, what, was that mysterious hidden quality in it; the power which was overcoming M'sieur Michel, stirring within him a turmoil that bewildered him?" (I, 186). Chopin frequently uses flowers to complete the Easter motifs in her stories, which also merge the liturgical and the agricultural seasons as major forces on the characters.

"With the Violin," "Madame Martel's Christmas Eve," and "A Matter of Prejudice" have Christmas as an organizing device. The last story is especially interesting because it suggests how integrated Catholicism was in the culture of New Orleans. The Creole Madame Carambeau disowns her son because he married an American woman. Madame, of course, lives in the Vieux Carre—now known as the French Quarter; her son lives in the American sector across Canal Street. Some years pass and an American child becomes ill during a party at Madame's, and the experience begins to move her to change as she wonders about her own "lost" grandchild and the prejudice which she has been harboring. On Christmas day she determines to attend Mass at the American cathedral rather than the French one. Afterwards, she visits her son in the American sector and discovers that the sick child is her granddaughter. Chopin combines the influences of a child visitor with the traditional power of the image of the Christ child to bring about a reunion of the family and the human spirit it represents.

"A Matter of Prejudice" describes accurately the sectionalism of New Orleans in the nineteenth century, and it also reveals the author's own difficulties in being accepted by the Chopin family. Her father-in-law, as Seyersted notes, "disliked her being half-Irish and he resented his son's decision to take her to live on the American side of the city."[3] Although the rejection was brief, the feelings which generated it obviously persisted, so that in *The Awakening* one finds that Edna's father does not approve her marrying a Catholic. In addition to her own experience, Chopin uses the agency of the Church and the ecclesiastical season as outward symbols of the good heart to solve the temporal problems which afflict the characters in this poignant tale.

Other stories also reveal diverse influences of Catholicism and Christianity. The Mass on a feast day and a Sunday is central to "Odalie Misses Mass" and "At Chênière Caminada." At the outset of the former, Chopin writes, "It was the fifteenth of August, the great feast of the Assumption, so generally observed in the Catholic parishes of Louisiana" (I, 406). The feast, also a part of the secular life of the region, forms the basis of the journey motif and the complication: a child with her dress selected especially for the day chooses not to accompany her family to the Mass but to keep an old black woman company. In the latter story the welling of a long unused organ, the chanting of the *Credo,* and the ringing of the *Angelus* signal the progress of romantic feelings in a young man for a beautiful, almost visionary, young woman whom he can never possess. The religious life provides the setting and contributes to the structure of "A Vocation and a Voice" and "Lilacs."[4] References to the Virgin range throughout Chopin's fiction—some of them pious and others cautious in tone.

French Louisiana has been the traditionally acknowledged source of much of Kate Chopin's fiction. In recent years some critics have hailed her development of female characters and associated themes as part of the contemporary feminist movement. Even more intrinsic to her literary works, however, is the pervasive influence of Catholicism and Christianity—forces which move her at once to conform and to rebel.

NOTES

[1]*Kate Chopin: A Critical Biography* (Baton Rouge: Louisiana State Univ. Press, 1969), p. 34. See also *A Kate Chopin Miscellany,* eds. Per Seyersted and Emily Toth (Natchitoches, La: Northwestern State Univ. Press, 1979), pp. 67–86.

[2]Kate Chopin, *The Complete Works of Kate Chopin,* ed. Per Seyersted (Baton Rouge: Louisiana State Univ. Press, 1969), I, 239. All further quotations from the fiction of Kate Chopin are from this edition, unless otherwise noted, and will hereafter be cited by volume and page in the text.

[3]Seyersted, *Critical Biography,* p. 37.

[4]See Elmo Howell, "Kate Chopin and the Pull of Faith: A Note on 'Lilacs,'" *Southern Studies,* 18 (1979), 103–09; also Thomas Bonner, Jr., "Kate Chopin's European Consciousness," *American Literary Realism, 1870–1910,* 8 (1975), 281–84.

Love, Death, and Faith in the New Orleans
Poets of Color

ALFRED J. GUILLAUME, JR.

In nineteenth-century antebellum New Orleans, there existed a social and cultural milieu unparalleled by that of any other Southern city. The people of New Orleans, the French, the Spanish, and the Americans, participated avidly in the cosmopolitan activities of the city. Theater, opera, concerts and balls were favorite pastimes.[1] Literature, much of it written in French, flourished.[2] The free people of color, *gens de couleur libres*, also figured prominently in the life of the city. These Creoles of Color, mixed-blood descendants of African and French and/or Spanish lineage, had certain social and civil liberties denied to slaves. They could acquire, transmit, and inherit property, and could serve as witnesses in civil suits involving whites and blacks. The right to sue whites and the right to trial were also unique privileges.[3]

The socio-political mobility of the free people of color vacillated, however, between fairly open access to the advantages of the white world and no access at all, as evidenced by legislation that sought to restrict their privileged status.[4] As their numbers increased and as they gained more economic stability, whites became less civil toward them and even intolerant. Caught between the dichotomy of being neither black nor white, the Creoles of Color felt the humiliation of a special kind of second class citizenship. No matter how far they advanced in refinement, culture, and economic independence, total integration into the majority world was denied them.

But in spite of numerous restrictive barriers, the free people of color still contributed significantly to the cultural life of New Orleans, not only as patrons of the visual and performing arts, but also as writers, journalists, painters, composers, musicians, sculptors and skilled artisans.[5] Many of these received the finest educa-

126

tion available. Some, like the poet Camille Thierry and the pianist-composer Edmond Dédé, studied in France; others attended private and parochial schools in the city or were tutored privately.[6] Educated in the classical tradition, they, along with their white counterparts, represented the intellectual elite of New Orleans society.

Among them developed a small literati who relished the written word. They met in salons to recite their literary creations, works that often imitated the French masters in style, form, theme, and content, and to assure publication of their work, they founded in 1843 the literary journal, *L'Album Littéraire des Jeunes Gens, Amateurs de Littérature.*[7] This short-lived publication was followed by a more ambitious project, a small volume of poetry, *Les Cenelles (Holly Berries)*, published in 1845.[8] Its editor and principal contributor, Armand Lanusse, envisioned this collective effort of seventeen poets as a contribution to art and also as a testimony to the benefits of the good humanistic education they had received.

Unfortunately, *Les Cenelles* is the only volume in which these poets published as a group. Although several continued to write, their later works appeared only in anthologies, journals, and newspapers. Two newspapers established by the free people of color, *L'Union* (1862–1864) and *La Tribune de la Nouvelle Orléans* (1864–1869), published most of their work after the antebellum period.[9] And after 1875, they published little. The Civil War had drastically changed the social and intellectual climate of New Orleans. The political concerns of both the black and white population left little time for leisure, and moreover, French as a literary expression had begun to fade, yielding its place to English.

The poems in *Les Cenelles* range in tone from light-hearted romantic ballads to dirges on death and suicide. Love's ecstasy and disillusionment are recurringly mirrored with romantic sentimentality and even effusion. The verses vary in lengths of 4, 5, 6, 8, 9, 10, and 12 syllables with several strophic forms, the most common versification being *abab* and *abba*.[10]

Reminiscent of the work of Lamartine, Hugo, and Béranger, French Romantic poets of the nineteenth century, these poems often portray an intimate dialogue between the poet and an

idealized nature. Love is exhilarating, an oasis of happiness.
Loving and being loved represent the zenith of earthly pleasure:

> O bonheur extrême
> Qu'ils sont beaux mes jours!
> Tu m'as dit: je t'aime!
> Redis-le toujours. . .
> (Michel St. Pierre, "Tu m'as dit Je t'aime")

> Que mon âme est ravie!
> Oh! que j'aime la vie
>   A tes côtés;
> Là, près du lac tranquille
> Vivons loin de la ville,
>   Loin des cités.

> Depuis que j'ai su plaire,
> Tout pour moi sur la terre
>   Est parfumé;
> Oui, tout semble sourire
> Alors que l'on peut dire:
>   Je suis aimé!
>   (Pierre Dalcour, "Au bord du lac")[11]

Les Cenelles is dedicated to "Louisianans of the Fair Sex":

> Veuillez bien accepter ces modestes Cenelles
> Que notre cœur vous offre avec sincerité;
> Qu'un seul regard tombe de vos chastes prunelles
> Leur tienne lieu de gloire et d'immortalité.
>   (Armand Lanusse)[12]

These charming Louisiana women, full of beauty and warmth, as
Lanusse describes them in his introductory remarks, are depicted
in contrasting images of angel, virgin, and goddess; flirt and coquette. They are pure, virtuous and gay, yet, at the same time, cruel
and fickle. They inspire happiness among admirers, who are
drunken with joy at the mere sight of them. The women are
"créole" in a few poems. One poet even speaks of his "blonde
créole."

The *Les Cenelles* women are the Petrarchan archetype of beauty
and charm. Their eyes, frequently blue, sparkle brightly. Their
luminous clarity radiates tenderness and joy. A suitor receiving one
glance from the eyes of his beloved is at once transformed into a
state of drunken ecstasy. If deprived of her love, the brilliance of

the beloved's eyes penetrates the dark recesses of his soul and
rekindles the burning flames of love:

> Car dans l'obscurité
> Souvent je ne rencontre
> Que la vive clarté
> Qui dans tes yeux se montre.
> (Armand Lanusse, "Les aman(t)s consolés")

. . . .

> Et je sens la vive étincelle
> Qui, s'échappant de sa prunelle,
> Soudain vient embraser mon cœur!
> (Pierre Dalcour, "Le chant d'amour")[13]

Equally inspiring is a smile from the beloved's lips that can capti-
vate the most timid suitor:

> Je te parlais, tu daignais me sourire;
> Heureux moments! je me croyais aux cieux.
> (B. Valcour, "Mon rêve")

> Mais la voilà! comme elle est embellie;
> Ah! que d'attraits, que d'aimables appas!
> Elle sourit,—combien elle est jolie!
> (Nelson Desbrosses, "Le retour au Village aux Perles")

> Viens, par ton doux sourire,
> Endormir mes douleurs. . .
> (Joanni Questy, "Vision")[14]

Her voice is seductive, melodic, pliant, captivating and enchanting.
The mellifluous sound of her voice is more natural and more beautiful than the sounds of Nature:

> Je crois aussi, dans mon délire,
> Entendre sa voix qui soupire
> Plus suave que le zéphyre
> Jouant à travers les rameaux,
> Et plus douce que le murmure
> Du clair ruisseau dont l'onde pure
> Serpente parmi les oiseaux.
> (Pierre Dalcour, "Le chant d'amour")[15]

A word graciously spoken lifts the paramour into a frenzied rapture
or blissful agony:

> Toujours ta voix enchanteresse
> Vient porter le trouble en mes sens;
> Je t'aime, hélas, avec ivresse,
> Toi qui causes tous mes tourments!
> Oh, mais je t'aime avec délire. . .
>   (Pierre Dalcour, "Les aveux")[16]

As virgin, embodying the virtues of purity and innocence, the Creole woman of color personifies the Ideal to which the poets aspire. Through her they communicate their innermost feelings of hope and felicity. She symbolizes integrity in a world with none. Her divine character is a source of strength and protection against human frailty:

> Car l'amour, l'amour seul d'une vierge adorée
> Peut consoler le cœur des maux qu'il a soufferts;
> C'est la frache oasis, c'est la manne sacrée,
> C'est la source d'eau pure au milieu des déserts!
>   (Pierre Dalcour, "Le chant d'amour")

> . . . c'est cette vertu qui s'oppose sans crainte
> Aux volontés d'un cœur impudique et vénal,
> Cette douce candeur, cette innocence empreinte
>   Sur ton front virginal.
>   (Michel-Ferdinand Liotau, "A Ida")[17]

No matter what fate he suffers at the beloved's whims, the poet remains faithful to the image of woman as the embodiment of perfection and inspiration. If separated from his sweetheart, he is melancholic. Her absence generates a void in poetic creativity; his lute no longer sings and his muse abandons him.

Generally, the suitor is shy, timid, and hesitant in his plea for love. He fears rejection:

> Je ne t'ai jamais dit: je t'aime,
> Ces mots à prononcer si doux!
> Craignant que mon amour extrême
> Soudain ne te mît en courroux . . .
>   (Pierre Dalcour, "Les aveux")[18]

If his love is rejected the adored virtuous beauty becomes a dispassionate flirt who through her coquette's manner receives pleasure in tormenting her lover. Her false promises of love cause extreme grief:

> Adieu promesses mensongères,
> Que tu me faisais si souvent!
> Oh! les femmes sont plus légères
> Que la feuille qui tourne au vent!
> (Pierre Dalcour, "A une inconstante")[19]

The happiness that love ostensibly offers has been recognized as deception, chimera.

The themes of love and death are closely connected in the poems of the free people of color. In many, the poet characteristically displays a childlike belief that happiness in love is eternal; the woman they laud, forever angelic and chaste. Deception, then, is a cruel blow. Death often appears as a natural end to rejected love. Life becomes meaningless, and as the poet J. Boise bitterly expresses in his poem about a disdained suitor, death is preferable to life without the beloved:

> Plus d'attrait, plus de charme,
> Tout est triste à mes yeux,
> Tout m'afflige et m'alarme,
> Le jour m'est odieux.
> Mes membres s'affaiblissent.—
> Que vais-je devenir?—
> Mes yeux s'appésantissent,
> Hélas! faut-il mourir!
> ("L'amant dédaigné")[20]

The lighter side of love is only occasionally seen. In B. Valcour's "Son chapeau et son schall," for example, the jealous paramour, wishing to keep the beauty of his beloved for his eyes only, is grateful for the protection that her bonnet and shawl afford from the admiring gaze of others:

> Chapeau chéri!
> Des yeux de mon amie,
> A mes rivaux, cache l'éclat si doux;
> Il porterait en leur âme ravie
> Le feu divin, et j'en serais jaloux,
> Chapeau chéri!
>
> . . . .
>
> Schall adoré!
> De sa taille divine

> Dérobe à tous les contours amoureux;
> Et ne permets qu'aucun regard devine
> Les biens cachés sous tes plis gracieux.
> Schall adoré![21]

The light-hearted tone mirrors the gay mood of the suitor, who, despite his jealousy, is perhaps secretly proud of the glances that his beautiful lady commands.

Married love is viewed as sacred and blissful, an enviable state. It is treated with humor, however, in a poem by Auguste Populus composed on the occasion of a friend's wedding. If read *aabb*, as originally written, it gives an entirely opposite view of marriage than when read *abab*:

> Ah! que l'homme a raison de s'estimer heureux
> Quand il a de l'hymen serré les chastes nœuds;
> Si dans le célibat il parcourt sa carrière,
> La larme chaque jour vient mouiller sa paupière.
> ("A mon ami P")[22]

Other poems treat marriage more seriously. In a poem by Numa Lanusse, the brother of Armand, the poet bestows his blessings of eternal happiness on a newlywed couple. Their love is viewed as supreme.

The Rosémines, Delphines, Herminas, Emmas, Coralies, and Coelinas of these verses are adored by a group of men who pay homage to the graceful beauty of Creole women. Curiously, references to the indignities of *plaçage* appear in only two poems. In one an old woman, before receiving penance, solicits the aid of a priest to "plaçer ma fille" (Armand Lanusse, "Epigramme"). In another, the poet bemoans the "liaisons impures" of young women who prostitute themselves for material gain (Armand Lanusse, "A Elora").[23]

Several poems treat the religious significance of death. Poems written on the death of a loved one—a friend, mother, sister, brother, or mentor—are not simply meaningless dirges on the end of someone's life, but charming and sincere pieces of religious sentiment that reveal the frailty of human existence and a belief in eternal happiness. For these Catholic poets, death is real; it is the portal to everlasting life with God. Man is dust and the pleasure of life ephemeral, but death offers hope. As it was for Hugo and other

French Romantics, for the Creole poets death is a personal experience. The pain of loss is intensely felt, but the poet's sorrow is diminished by submitting his grief to God's will. When Armand Lanusse laments the death of his brother, his faith that they will meet again in Heaven assuages his bereavement:

> "Non, je ne doute de ce divin mystère:
> Nous devons tous au ciel, un jour, nous réunir.
> Tranquilles et conten(t)s auprès de notre mère,
> D'un bonheur éternel là nous pourrons jouir.—
> Au revoir, mon cher frère!
> ("Un frère")[24]

Bitterness is seldom expressed, but regret is voiced when a death is felt to be premature. Such is the case in a poem by Joanni Questy mourning the death of the poet William Stephen. Didactic in tone, the poem is rich in images of the uncertainty of life:

> Oh! dors, oui, dors toujours jusqu'au jour solennel!
> Et quand la nuit éteint la grande voix du monde;
> Que Celui que je sers d'un doux regard m'inonde.
> Je te lègue ces chants, hommage fraternel,
> Etincelle ravie au foyer de mon âme
> Pour dorer ton oubli d'une rapide flamme.
>
> Dors, dors toujours! que rien ne trouble ton sommeil;
> Sur ta tombe cachée aux rayons de soleil,
> Qu'un saule tristement épande son ombrage;
> Qu'un marbre où les regrets auront gravé ton nom,
> Puisse dire au passant: "Il est mort avant l'âge,
> Derrière lui laissant un lumineux sillon."
> ("Une larme")[25]

If bitterness is indeed expressed, pardon from God is immediately asked. Michel-Ferdinand Liotau, lamenting the death of a newly born daughter, quietly resigns himself to accept the death as God's will:

> De ce monde, grand Dieu, que meut ta volonté,
> Ainsi tu fis le but et la diversité.
> Que mon cœur soit brisé par cet arrêt sévère;
> Tu l'as voulu, Seigneur, je n'ai plus qu'à me taire!—
> Il faut m'y conformer, reçois donc mes adieux,
> O toi dont l'âme pure est maintenant aux cieux!
> ("Un an après")[26]

This unquestioning submission to God's will can be explained only by the Creole poets' faith that death is not final, but simply a new beginning. The tranquility and happiness it promises is even envied as in Michel St. Pierre's lovely poem, "La jeune fille mourante," where life is shown to be deceitful, hope elusive, and love cruel:

> Que ton sort est heureux, qu'il est digne d'envie!
> Jeune fille tu pars, tu quittes cette vie,
> Tu vas jouir en paix dans un séjour meilleur
> Emportant avec toi, l'innocence et l'honneur!
> Va, ne regrette rien, la voix de Dieu t'appelle,
> Sans larmes ni soupirs envole-toi vers elle;
> Rien n'est sûr ici-bas, le plaisir est trompeur,
> L'espoir est fugitif ainsi que le bonheur![27]

Each death scene is carefully orchestrated. The dying person makes a feeble attempt to hold on to life, but as the spirit bravely yields to death, those around the bed accept the loss, their grief mitigated by belief in Heaven:

> Ta voix avec effort, par la douleur brisée,
> Murmure enfin le nom de notre rédempteur;
> La main sur son image en ce moment posée,
> Tu demandes, sans doute, à ce divin Seigneur
> Que ton âme soit délivrée!—
> . . . .
> O ciel! je vois déjà se fermer ta paupière!
> La mort inexorable a réclamé ses droits!
> Tu ne seras bientôt qu'une froide pouissière!
> Adieu, ma mère, adieu pour la dernière fois.—
> Que la terre te soit légère!
> (Armand Lanusse, "Une mère mourante")
>
> Adieu—je vois la mort qui s'apprête et s'avance—
> Ton regard s'obscurcit—chacun frémit d'avance—
> Encore un seul instant, encore un seul soupir,—
> Et tu ne sera plus que cendre et souvenir!
> Adieu donc pour toujours, . . .
> ("La jeune fille mourante")[28]

In all of the verses quoted above, death peacefully comes. Human will yields to divine will.

But this serene portrayal of death is by no means the only view represented in the poetry of the New Orleans people of color.

Suicide, also a prominent theme of French Romantic poetry, is vividly present. The theme appears in two poems by Camille Thierry, "L'ombre d'Eugène B." and "Le suicide." In the first, the soul of a youth who has killed himself pleads for his friends to join his mother in prayer so that his soul may be received by God. In "Le suicide" the poet, preparing to take his life, describes the frailty of life with a powerful nautical image. A tiny boat ("frêle esquif") is battered by the winds of a storm at sea:

> La vie est un affreux rivage;
> On craint trop d'en quitter le bord:
> Frêle esquif battu par l'orage
> Dois-je pâlir devant la mort?[29]

The fear of death is finally replaced by a realization that death is the sole solution to life's misery. The poet regrets only that he will leave his mother with no one to comfort her in her old age, and for that reason, he asks forgiveness. He does not fear Hell, but as a Creole Catholic is confident that he will await her before the tribunal of God.

A later poem "2 novembre" by Adolphe Duhart, published in *La Tribune* in 1867, commemorates All Souls' Day, a day set aside by the Church to pray for the souls of the deceased. The poem opens with a somber meditation on the significance of November 2, in which Christians are reminded of their annual obligation to pray for the dead. In the first three stanzas, November 2 is referred to as "le jour sans soleil," "la nuit froide et sombre," "le jour des regrets," "la nuit de tristesses," "le jour de prière," and "la nuit des morts." Death is the "souveraine et immuable loi." The fatalism of the images ominously recalls the final hour, the universal reality that all men will die: "Heure sombre où chacun tristement songera/"Qu'ici l'homme est poussière et poussière sera."[30]

The suddenness of death is compared to the unexpected eruption of thunder and lightning on a quiet, sunny day. This realization of death necessitates a spiritual preparation for the end. The poet admonishes all of us, then, to pray:

> A genoux donc!. . .Prions pour ceux qui sont passés,
> Et dont, sur les chemins, les pas sont effacés.

> Enfant, femme, vieillard, et toi, grand de la terre,
> Dans l'enceinte sacrée et toujours solitaire,
> Qui que tu sois enfin, à genoux! à genoux!
> Prie en ton cœur pour toi; implore pour nous![31]

In the stanzas that follow, death as leveler is evoked, a death that effaces all distinction between people, striking the rich and the poor, the powerful and the weak. Because of the revered role that women hold as lady, wife and mother, the poet asks them to intercede to God for the souls of others:

> Toi, femme, épouse et mère, ô trinité sacrée
> Toi, dont toute prière au ciel est révérée,
> Demande avec la foi grâce au juge eternel
> Pour l'enfant qui sourit à ton sein maternel,
> Pour le pécheur qui court vers un fugitif leurre,
> Pour le maudit qui hurle, et pour celui qui pleure . . .[32]

Manifest throughout the poem is the poet's sincere wish that all mankind obtain salvation. This poem echoes the sentiment expressed in the *Les Cenelles* poems on death that eternal salvation awaits the faithful. The poem ends, however, with a universal plea that we remember the dead in our prayers.

As the poems on death indicate, faith in God is profoundly important for the Creole poets of color. Nothing seems to diminish their faith, neither rejection in love nor the loss of a loved one. To the contrary, tragedy increases their fervor. In the love poems, the poets universally plead to God for comfort. Exclamations of "Mon Dieu," commonly used, are colored with sorrow and hope. Brooding and bemoaning their fate, they seek God to alleviate their misery. A charming poem by Joanni Questy, "Prière," which appeared in *L'Album Littéraire* 1 August 1843, is a fine example of their unwavering belief in God's goodness. As the title suggests, the poem is a prayer. The poet, crushed by the struggles of his daily life, pleads for deliverance from his sufferings. In the first quatrain, he addresses the Lord directly through the imperative "Donnez-moi" (Give me). Weary of conflicts, he seeks peace, represented by the word "palme" (palm leaf). In the third quatrain, the poet is acutely aware that his only hope lies with God: "Mon Dieu! je n'espérais qu'en vous!" Curiously, in the fourth quatrain, the imperative changes from the polite form reserved for strangers to the familiar form used for persons with whom one is well acquainted (Donnez . . . Mets . . .):

> Donnez-moi donc un sommeil calme,
> Un jour de joie et de bonheur;
> Après les combats vient la palme,
>   Pourtant Seigneur!
>
> .   .   .   .
>
> Hélas! mon Dieu! fais qu'une étoile
> Eclaire mon noir hori(z)on!
> Mets à ma nef déjà sans voile
>   Un aviron.[33]

This change is indicative, perhaps, of the strength that the poet has received as a result of prayer. He is more comfortable with God and more confident that God will help him. The last two quatrains offer hope as the poem ends with an "Amen" ("Ainsi soit-il").

Michel-Ferdinand Liotau, in his poem "Un comdamné à mort," realistically portrays how faith in God can change desperation into hope. Condemned to die, a despondent prisoner, locked in a dark cell for ten days, seeks the comfort of God; he prays that in spite of his unworthiness he will merit God's goodness:

> Oh! si du condamné l'arrêt est trop certain,
> Bénis-moi, mon Seigneur, bénis-moi de ta main.
> Fais-moi donc oublier, si la mort me réclame,
> Tous ces pensers affreux qui me torturent l'âme;
> Laissi-moi mériter, ô Seigneur, tu bouté,
> Qui protège toujours la faible humanité.[34]

As the condemned man prepares to die, he unselfishly begs God's blessing for humanity as well as for himself.

Traditionally Catholic, the free people of color were active participants in the Church.[35] Their love for their religion is reflected in another of Liotau's poems, "Une impression." The poet laments the neglect and deterioration of St. Louis Church (now St. Louis Cathedral). He nostalgically recalls the days when its parishioners flocked to attend services. The mysticism that accompanied many of the liturgical services is sadly evoked. His own baptism is remembered. Choked with emotion, the poet prays for harmony among people, for an end to the strife that causes hatred and discord:

> Puisque jamais en vain nous prions le Seigneur,
> Chrétiens, unissons-nous; quand ce Dieu tutélaire
> A versé tout son sang pour nous sur le Calvaire,
> Espérons qu'en ce jour lui seul puissant et fort,
> En le priant du cœur changera notre sort;
> Prions si nous voulons que sa miséricorde
> Détruise parmi nous la haine et la discorde.[36]

These verses also allude indirectly to the racial dissidence caused by the precarious socio-political status of the *gens de couleur libres*, outcasts in a society in which they were denied full participation.

In the *Les Cenelles* poems most of the romantic themes are presented. Emotion is extolled, and there is a strong preoccupation with self as the poets are mired in melancholy sentiment. Nature is idealized; the poets, pariahs, withdraw from reality and create a fanciful world of imagined happiness. The women they laud represent goodness and candor in a world of deceit. Death and love are their only avenues to God. Conspicuously absent, however, are references to the reality of the poets' lives. The poems ignore it. Nor is there any indication of racial awareness. The poems could, in fact, have been written by white Creoles or natives of France. Except for Liotau's poem about St. Louis Cathedral, there are just two other fragments of local color—Canal Carondelet in a poem by Camille Thierry and Bayou Road in a poem by Nelson Desbrosses. In this respect, the New Orleans poets of color differed from the French Romantics whose melancholy dirges abound in local color.

How can one explain this absence of psychological and public reality? The most plausible explanation, of course, lies with race. At the time of *Les Cenelles*'s publication, literature that might incite discontent among the colored populace was prohibited,[37] and so the poets, whatever their true feelings about the city and their place in it, could write nothing of daily experience. As a result they sought refuge and an outlet for their talent in the typical romantic themes of love, women, nature and personal sadness. It is perhaps only in an imagery more somber and sad even than that of the great French Romantics that their true feelings can be detected.

Although much of the later poetry of the Creoles of color reiter-
ated the major romantic themes, the work published in *L'Union* and
La Tribune presents poets eager to confront their social reality
more directly. Poems are contemporary in subject matter. Slavery,
the Civil War, and racial attitudes are now central themes. "Il n'est
pas" of Armand Lanusse, published in *La Tribune* in 9 September
1866 is a good example. Dedicated to the Creole poet identified
simply as Antony, the poem, in roll-call fashion, lists the kinds of
individuals for whom God does not exist. Among many evildoers
mentioned is the priest who uses his pulpit to preach racial dishar-
mony:

> Non, il n'existe pas pour ce ministre oblique
> Qui prétend le servir, et méprise sa loi;
> Ni pour ce faux chrétien, ce prêtre catholique
> Qui veut qu'un préjugé soit article de foi.[38]

The poem concludes with the statement that God is for a selected
few—those who do not give in to the pleasures of the time.

Unquestionably, the literature of the *gens de couleur libres* is
important in New Orleans cultural history. The Lanusses, Questys,
and Thierrys left new generations a legacy unique in this country.
That they wrote in French and looked to France for their inspiration is crucial to understanding their aesthetic. The New Orleans
Creole poets, as Charles Hamlin Good observes, represent the
"first American Negro literary movement."[39] Their journal,
L'Album Littéraire, was the first American black literary publication. Their newspaper, *La Tribune,* became the first Negro daily
newspaper in the United States.[40]

One must observe that much of this poetry is monotonous, deriv-
ative, and repetitive in sentiment. Nevertheless, it has charm and
remains a monument for succeeding generations as Lanusse hoped
that it would. Such is the judgment also of a review of *Les Cenelles*
that appeared in *La Chronique* in 30 January 1848:

> La poésie légère de nos jours a le défaut d'être trop personelle; il n'y est
> le plus souvent question que des sentimen(t)s et des passions de celui
> qui écrit. Quelques uns des plus grands poètes du siècle, tels que Hugo
> et Lamartine, ne sont point eux-mêmes à l'abri du reproche; mais Hugo

se fait pardonner ce cachet intime et égoiste par les hardiesses de sa
pensée et le coloris de son vers, et Lamartine par les harmonies infinies
de son style.

Cette tendance du jour va souvent jusqu'à l'exagération; et l'on devine
sans peine que l'enthousiasme public n'y gagne` pas beaucoup. *Les
Cenelles* auraient pu aisément éviter cet écueil, puisqu'elles sont
l'œuvre collective de plusieurs personnes. Mais évidemment chacun
paya à son insu le tribut du siècle, et, après, que chaque poète eut
apporté son contingent au recueil, il se trouva que tous avaient changé à
peu près sur la même corde. *Les Cenelles* manquent donc essentielle-
ment de variété. Nous ne cherchons point à déguiser notre pensée au
moyen de subterfuges de style, puisque nous pouvons ajouter que, mal-
gré la monotonie du sentiment, nous avons passé de doux momen(t)s à
feuilleter la plupart de ces aimables poésies.[41]

A harsh but equally favorable judgment is offered by Charles
Testut, a contemporary of the poets of color, in his *Portraits
littéraires de la Nouvelle Orléans* published in New Orleans in
1850. Included in a discussion of several literary figures are
Thierry, Questy and Lanusse. Although he calls their poetry monotonous, he nevertheless finds it refreshing. Their only fault,
in Testut's opinion, is that they published little.[42]

Had these poets been more prolific in their writing, their poetic
themes would probably have been more diverse and in all likeli-
hood they would have developed a style of their own. That they
published at all is a remarkable achievement when one considers
the time and place in which their literature was written.

NOTES

[1]New Orleans was as rowdy as it was genteel. Gambling and cock fights were also
popular pastimes. For more information on the cultural and social history of nineteenth-century New Orleans, consult: Loren Schweninger, "A Negro Sojourner in
Antebellum New Orleans," *Louisiana History* 20 (Summer 1979), 304–15; John
Blasingame, *Black New Orleans, 1860–1880* (Chicago: Univ. of Chicago Press,
1973), Ch. 1; Ira Berlin, *Slaves Without Masters: The Free Negro in the Antebellum
South* (New York: Pantheon Books, 1974), pp. 135–342; David Rankin, "The Forgot-
ten People: Free People of Color in New Orleans, 1850–1870," Diss. John Hopkins
University 1976; H. E. Sterkx, *The Free Negro in Ante-Bellum Louisiana* (Ruther-
ford: Fairleigh Dickinson Univ. Press, 1972).

[2]For a more complete discussion of the development of French literature in
Louisiana, consult: Ruby Van Allen Caulfield, *The French Literature of Louisiana*
(New York: Columbia Univ., 1929); Edward Larocque Tinker, *Les Ecrits de langue
française en Louisiane au XIXe siècle* (Paris, 1932); Reginald Hamel, *La Louisiane (Créole) (1762–1900): Littérature politique et sociale* (Montréal: Universi-
té de Montréal, 1977).

[3]Annie Lee West Stahl, "The Free Negro in Ante-Bellum Louisiana," *Louisiana Historical Quarterly*, 25 (1942), 312–36; Paul A. Kunkel, "Modifications in Louisiana Negro Legal Status Under Louisiana Constitutions, 1812–1957," *Journal of Negro History*, 44 (1959), 1–25; Donald E. Everett, "Free Persons of Color in Colonial Louisiana," *Louisiana History*, 7 (1966), 21–50; Charles B. Roussève, *The Negro in Louisiana: Aspects of His History and His Literature* (1937; rpt. New York: Johnson Reprints, [1970]), Ch. 3; Alice Dunbar-Nelson, "People of Color in Louisiana," *Journal of Negro History*, 1 (1916), 361–76, II (1917), 51–78.

[4]Stahl, p. 335.

[5]Rodolphe Lucien Desdunes, *Our People and Our History*, trans. Sister Dorothea Olga McCants (Baton Rouge: Louisiana State Univ. Press, 1973). The book was originally published in Montreal in 1911 under the title *Nos Hommes et Notre Histoire*.

[6]Betty Porter, "The History of Negro Education in Louisiana," *Louisiana Historical Quarterly*, 25 (1942), 728–821; Nathan Willey, "Education of the Colored Population of Louisiana," *Harper's New Monthly Magazine*, 33 (1866), pp. 244–50; Marie Dejan, "Education for Negroes in New Orleans Prior to 1915," Master's thesis, Xavier University of Louisiana, 1941; Roussève, pp. 42–44; Desdunes, Chs. vi, vii, viii.

[7]J.-L. Marciacq, whose racial identity is unclear, was the editor, but it was probably Armand Lanusse who served as the motivating force behind the journal's publication. See Roussève, pp. 63–65; Tinker, pp. 296–98.

[8]On the meaning of *Les Cenelles*'s title, Roussève offers this explanation: "Its title, the name of the fruit of the hawthorn, from whose thorny shrub come fragrant blossoms, bespeaks the modesty of its authors, and was probably chosen to suggest under what trying circumstances and in how decidedly unfavorable an environment its eighty-two poems were composed and published." pp. 67–68.

A centennial edition of *Les Cenelles* was published in 1945, Edward Maceo Coleman, ed., *Creole Voices: Poems in French by Free Men of Color First Published in 1845* (Washington, D.C.: Associated Publishers). Recently, a translation of *Les Cenelles* was published, Régine Latortue, et al. *Les Cenelles: A Collection of Poems by Creole Writers of the Early Nineteenth Century* (Boston: G. K. Hall, 1979).

[9]Charles Hamlin Good, "The First American Negro Literary Movement," *Opportunity*, March 1932, pp. 76–79; H. Carrington Lancaster, "French Poetry by Men of Color Published in New Orleans in 1845," *The American Society Legion of Honor Magazine*, Spring 1947, pp. 55–66; Joan R. Sherman, *Invisible Poets: Afro-Americans of the Nineteenth Century*, (Chicago: Univ. of Illinois Press, 1974), p. 251.

[10]Other French language newspapers also occasionally published work by the free people of color: *L'Abeille, Le Courier de la Louisiane, La Chronique, La Renaissance Louisianais, Le Dimanche, L'Orléanais*, to name a few.

[11]Oh! Sublime happiness/How beautiful are my days!/You told me: I love you!/Say it always . . . ("You Told Me, I Love You"); Oh!How happy I am!/How I love life when I am at your side!/ There, near the tranquil lake,/Let's live far from town, far from cities. From the moment I became aware of love,/Everything on earth was filled with fragrance./Yes, everything seems to smile when one can truthfully say:/I am loved! ("On the Edge of the Lake"). All translations are mine. The poems are from *Les Cenelles*, unless noted differently.

[12]Graciously accept these modest fruit/That our hearts sincerely offer you;/May a single glance from your pure and chaste brow,/ Bring to them the glory of immortality.

[13]Often in the darkness/I encounter only/The vivid clarity/That radiates in your

eyes. ("The Consoled Lovers"); I feel the warm spark/That falls from her brow/ Suddenly reach to embrace my heart! ("Song of Love").

[14]You deigned to smile as I spoke to you;/Oh! What a happy moment! I thought I was in Heaven. ("My Dream"); There she is!Oh!How beautiful!/Ah! What appeal, what charm!/She smiles— What loveliness! ("Return to the Village of Pearls"); Come, put all sorrows to rest/With your sweet smile. ("Vision").

[15]In my delirium, I believe/I hear the sighs of her voice/More gentle than the wind/Whistling across the branches,/And softer than the murmur of a clear stream/ Whose pure ripples wind/Gently among the birds ("Song of Love").

[16]Your enchanting voice/Always troubles my senses;/But I love you madly,/You, who cause all my sorrows/Oh, I love you deliriously . . . ("The Avowals").

[17]Only the love of an adored virgin/Can cure the heart of the wrongs it has suffered;/Such love is a cool oasis, the sacred manna,/ The source of fresh water in the middle of the desert! ("Song of Love"); It's that virtue that opposes without fear/The desires of an immodest and impure heart,/That sweet candor, that innocence imprinted/On your virginal face ("To Ida").

[18]I never told you that I loved you,/Those words too sweet to pronounce!/I feared that my deep love/Would make you angry . . . ("The Avowals").

[19]Goodbye, false promises,/That you so often made!/Oh! Women are flightier/Than the leaves that fly in the wind! ("To Someone Unfaithful").

[20]Life is no longer alluring and charming,/Everything is shrouded in sadness./ Everything distresses and frightens me./Even the sunshine is repugnant./My body is growing weak./What will become of me?/My eyes are becoming heavy./Oh! I must die! ("The Rejected Paramour").

[21]Lovely hat!/Hide the soft brillance of my beloved's eyes/From my rivals./It will bring the divine fire of love to their delighted soul/And I will be jealous/Lovely hat! Precious shawl!/Hide from everyone the delicate contours of her heavenly figure;/ And let no one see/The treasures hidden under your gracious folds./Precious shawl! ("Her Hat and Her Shawl").

[22]Ah! Man has every reason to believe himself happy/When he enters the bonds of matrimony;/During his bachelor days, courting the ladies,/A tear wet his eyelid everyday. If read *abab:* Ah! Man has every reason to believe himself happy/During his bachelor days, courting the ladies,/When he enters the bonds of matrimony/ A tear wets his eyelid everyday ("To My Friend P.").

[23]Many white Creoles formed sexual liaisons with free women of color. In many instances these gentlemen maintained two separate households, one for the white family and another for the black family. Children born of such unions often became the heirs of their white fathers.

These *plaçages* usually developed at the quadroon balls where whites courted the beautiful ladies of color. Free men of color were not allowed to attend, Stahl, pp. 305–312.

[24]No, I don't doubt this sacred mystery:/One day, we will meet again in Heaven./ Peaceful and happy near our mother,/There, we will find eternal happiness./Goodbye, my dear brother! ("A Brother").

[25]Oh! Sleep, yes, sleep forever until the eternal day!/And when night silences the great voice in the world/May He whom I serve shower me with a kind glance./In order to gild your passing/I bequeath these songs to you/Bright spark in the recesses of my soul,/A brotherly tribute. Sleep, sleep forever! May nothing trouble your sleep!/On your tomb hidden from the rays of the sun,/A willow sadly spreads its shade./May the stone where sorrow will have engraved your name,/Say to the passerby: "He died before time,/ Leaving behind him a brilliant path."

[26]May your will be done on earth, Almighty God./Thus you add purpose and variety to life./Oh! how my heart is torn by this harsh decree;/It's your will, Lord,/I

should not complain!/My will is your will./Receive my goodbyes,/You whose chaste soul is now in Heaven! ("One Year Later").

[27]Oh, how blessed is your fate! It's worthy of envy!/Child, you are leaving this life,/You are going to enjoy peace in a better place/ Bringing with you innocence and honor!/Go, don't regret anything, the voice of God calls you,/Without tears or sighs, hasten to Him;/ Nothing on earth is certain, pleasure is deceitful;/Hope and happiness are elusive ("The Dying Girl").

[28]Your voice, weakened with sorrow/Murmurs finally and with great effort, the name of our Savior;/With your hand resting on His image,/You ask the divine Lord/ That your soul be taken! Oh! Heaven! I see your eyes begin to close!/Indomitable death has claimed its rights!/You will soon be just cold dirt!/Goodbye, Mother. Goodbye for the last time!/ May you be relieved of your earthly burdens! ("A Dying Mother"); Goodbye! I see death preparing to come./Your eyes become cloudy. Everyone shudders prematurely./Still one instant, still one sigh,/And you will be no more than ashes and a memory!/Goodbye, forever! ("The Dying Girl").

[29]Life is a ghastly shore;/One unduly fears to leave its borders:/ Frail skiff battered by the storm,/Should I turn pale facing death?

[30]"day without sunshine," "day of sorrows," "cold and somber night," "night of sadness," "day of prayer," "night of the dead." "Sovereign and resolute law." Somber hour when everyone dreams/"That on earth, man is dust and into dust he will return."

[31]Kneel! Let us pray for those who have passed,/For those whose feet are erased on the paths./Child, woman, old man, and you, mighty of the earth,/In the sacred and solitary walls of this cemetery,/Whoever you might be, kneel! kneel!/Pray sincerely for yourself! Beg mercy for us!

[32]You, woman, wife and mother, oh, holy trinity,/You, whose every prayer is revered in Heaven,/With faith, ask the eternal judge for grace/For the smiling child nursing at your breast,/For the sinner who runs toward an elusive delusion,/For the wretched who cry out, and for those who weep.

[33]Do give me a restful sleep,/A day of joy and happiness;/After combat comes the palm branch, Lord!/Alas! my God! Let a star/ Brighten my dark horizon;/Place an oar on my ship/Already with sails ("Prayer").

[34]If the decree of a condemned man is so certain,/Bless me, O Lord, bless me with your hand./If death claims me, make me forget then/All these horrible thoughts that torture my soul./Permit me, O Lord, to merit your goodness/That protects forever feeble humanity ("A Prisoner Condemned to Death").

[35]The free people of color attended St. Louis Cathedral and St. Augustine Church in large numbers. Half of the pews in St. Augustine were rented by the people of color, André Lafargue, p. 686.

[36]Since our prayers to the Lord are never in vain,/Christians, let us unite; God, our Guardian/Shed his blood for us on Calvary;/Let us hope that He, the most powerful and strong/Will hear our prayer and change our lot./Let us pray if we want His mercy/To destroy among us hatred and strife.

[37]Stahl, p. 334.

[38]No, He does not exist for this aberrant minister/Who pretends to serve God, and disobeys His law;/Nor for the false Christian, this Catholic priest/Who preaches that prejudice ought to be a doctrine of faith.

[39]Good, p. 76.

[40]Roussève, p. 119.

[41]The frivolous poetry of today has the fault of being too personal; it is no longer a question of the sentiments and passions of those who write it. Some of the great poets of our time, such as Hugo and Lamartine, are not beyond reproach. But Hugo and Lamartine can be forgiven for this intimate and egotistical stylishness, Hugo,

because of the depth of his thought and the brilliance of his verse, Lamartine, because of the infinite harmonies of his style.

The tendency of today's poetry is toward exaggeration, and one can readily ascertain that the public does not gain much from it. *Les Cenelles* could easily have avoided this stumbling block, particularly, since it is the collective work of several poets. But evidently, each one unknowingly imitated the style of the time. After each poet's work was published in the volume, it appears that they all sang the same tune. Essentially then, *Les Cenelles* lacks variety. We do not attempt to disguise our thoughts through subterfuges of style, because we can add that in spite of the monotony of sentiment, we spent enjoyable moments paging through most of these lovely poems.

[42]Testut befriended the poets of color and included a poem by Camille Thierry in a volume of his own verse, *Fleurs d'Ete,* published in New Orleans in 1851.

Alfred Mercier, French Novelist of New Orleans

GEORGE REINECKE

With some doubts I resurrect Alfred Mercier and the small literary world he represented. Louisiana French literature was never great and only sometimes good. Perhaps it might be better to let the folk imagination as exemplified in the tourist trade replace the genuine variety of Louisiana French life and language in the nineteenth century with the stereotypes of the fun-loving primitive in the swamps, the gambling, dueling planter, and the swooning crino-lined womenfolk. Many of the descendants of the New Orleans bourgeoisie and Mississippi planters are themselves quite unaware of the more factual details concerning the little French melting pot which was South Louisiana in the last century. Here Blacks, Indians, Irish, Germans, Spaniards and a variety of others blended into a Creole culture, in which all used one or another variety of French—Acadian, Antillean Creole, or French colonial. In New Orleans especially we find all sorts of evidence of past literacy. The French theater and opera prospered. Countless daily and weekly French newspapers appeared, and though most soon vanished, new ones came to take their places. The daily *Abeille* continued publication for nearly a century. French schools were numerous, and the prosperity of the pre-war era allowed many to send their sons to France for a higher education.

Of the several hundred writers named by Edward Larocque Tinker in his bio-bibliography, *Les Ecrits de langue française en Louisiane au XIX⁰ siècle*, many were either occasional poets or writers on a variety of prosaic subjects, ranging from arithmetic to medicine to vegetable gardening. But quite a few attempted litera-ture as we know it, and among these there were at least a dozen writers of some substance: the Rouquette brothers, Charles Testut, Charles Gayarré, Placide Canonge, Armand Garreau, Mme. Sidonie de la Houssaye, Victor Séjour, Albert Delpit, the Dessommes brothers, Edward and George, and Alcée Fortier. Among the latter group, pride of place must surely be awarded to the polymath Alfred Mercier.

Though Mercier was a practicing physician holding the doctorate of the faculty of Paris, his chief efforts throughout the second half of his long life were aimed at marshalling the forces of French in his native state and leading the struggle by example. He thus became in the post-war era the leader of French literary efforts in the state as founder and secretary of the *Athenée Louisianais* and editor of *Les Comptes-rendus,* its important magazine, which Lafcadio Hearn at least found comparable in content and interest to the best English magazines of the United States. For this periodical he wrote over two decades a great number of articles on topics as varied as nihilism, pugilism, earthquakes and philology, to say nothing of contemporary French literature. He welcomed young writers such as Fortier and the Dessommes to its pages and coaxed others to become writers for the first time. But at the same moment, he was busying himself with a succession of novels and verse publications.

Mercier's literary career falls into two distinct portions, and it is with the second and more important of these, the Louisiana part, that we are here concerned. Born just a year after Andrew Jackson's victory at Chalmette, Mercier grew up in his native Jefferson Parish, just opposite New Orleans, and learned the Creole before he could speak standard French. In his early teens, however, he was sent to Paris to be educated at the Collège Louis-le-Grand, the chief preparatory school for the University of Paris. He remained in Paris for about eight years before returning to New Orleans. He then went to Boston for a time to improve his English. By 1842 he was back in Paris with enough verse in hand to make a book, published by Bouis in that year. This first significant publication contained two long romantic poems, the very titles of which suggest the influences of Chateaubriand and Byron: *L'Ermite du Niagara* and *La Rose de Smyrne.* To these was added a collection of lyric verse that he called *Erato.* Just how Alfred Mercier spent his time during the next five years is not clear. He seems to have remained in France except for trips into various parts of western Europe. We know for certain that in 1847 he undertook a voyage on foot through Italy into Sicily with several of his artistic Parisian friends and his young nephew, Nelvil Soulé, son of Pierre Soulé, Louisiana's French-born senator, whose biography Mercier was to publish the next year (*Biographie de Pierre Soulé, Senateur à Washington,* Paris: Dentu, 1848). This unhurried trip to Sicily was to have a marked influence on Mercier's later fiction. It is rather clear that the maturing Mercier (he was already thirty-two) busied himself in academic study and in the literary life of cafés and salons. Many of his associates seem to have been members of the radical democratic parties who initiated the revolution against Louis-Philippe in 1848, only to see the Second Republic lose out almost immediately to Louis-Napoleon.

One of the democratic organs of Paris was *La Réforme,* which also conducted a publishing house. Mercier had composed a fiction, first in dramatic form—he hoped to have it acted by the Comédie Française—and then, when this did not work out, in the style of the sensational novels frequently serialized in French (and New Orleans) newspapers, partaking of the style of Dumas and the now-forgotten Eugène Sue, author of *The Wandering Jew* and *The Mysteries of Paris.* The play seems to have been entitled *Auri-Fames* (i.e., money-hunger). In its narrative form the play became *Auri-Fames, ou l'Avare de New-York,* but *La Réforme* had its offices burned in the course of the revolutionary struggles during the very week when the book was to be published. When the revolution failed of its aims, Mercier, who had written about its progress for a New Orleans newspaper, *La Chronique,* accompanied young Soulé back to New Orleans, but soon returned to Paris. At about this point in his life he seems to have resolved to abandon literature, apparently destroying a poem called *Oceola,* a satire, *Le Sacre de Belgrave-Square,* and another work of unspecified genre, *Les Queues de Chevaux* (Horse Tails). Whether or not *Auri-Fames* in both dramatic and narrative form was likewise destroyed is uncertain. The play is now lost, and a copy of the novel was destroyed, although the tale later saw print as *Hénoch Jédésias* in post-Civil War New Orleans. It has been said that Mercier reworked the story from memory, but the other account, that a copy of the original romance had survived in the hands of a friend, seems the more likely.

Shortly thereafter, Mercier married his Parisian landlord's daughter and in his thirty-third year began the study of medicine. When he was thirty-nine he obtained his degree, and threw himself into the practice of his profession, returning to New Orleans with wife and children and helping to form the New Orleans Medical Society. Unhappy now in his native city, he returned to France and served as a doctor first with a factory in southern Normandy, then in one of the less elegant quarters of suburban Paris. For years he kept his vow to give up literature. Indeed, the first non-medical subject to appear under his name after he made his resolve was a pamphlet urging the French government to aid the Southern Confederacy (1863).

Perhaps the war wiped out Mercier's additional income; perhaps he believed he could live more comfortably in a nation without slavery than he had in the pre-war South. Whatever the case, the heretofore restless doctor moved his family in about 1865 once more to New Orleans, there to remain until his death twenty-eight years later, practicing medicine, writing, editing, and serving as a rallying point for the continuation of French in Louisiana.

It is with this period, and specifically with the five novels he wrote and published in New Orleans, that this article is chiefly concerned. *Hénoch Jédésias* is not considered because it seems likely that it belongs *in toto* to the first phase of Mercier's literary work, though published in 1869 in *L'Epoque*, a New Orleans weekly newspaper. As the titles might suggest, the work is a strange mixture of Monte Cristo and Shylock, the main figure being an immensely rich and powerful New York Jewish banker. Mercier republished it in the pages of his *Comptes-rendus* in 1892 and 1893, seemingly unchanged, judging from the few surviving installments of *L'Epoque*.

The New Orleans novels of Mercier include *Le Fou de Palerme* (1873), *Lidia* (1873), *La Fille du Prêtre* (in three volumes, 1877–78), *L'Habitation Saint-Ybars* (1881), and *Johnelle* (1891), all of which are available in the Howard-Tilton Library of Tulane University. Not only the barrier of language but also the relative inaccessability of Mercier's works makes it useful to summarize the plots. Reviewing the novels in chronological order will also indicate Mercier's stylistic development.

Le Fou de Palerme (The Madman of Palermo)

Larocque Tinker rather naively took this novella for an account of genuine events learned at second hand by Mercier when he visited Palermo in 1847. The romantic nature of the events it narrates pretty well precludes this possibility. Though the Louisianian doubtless visited the gardens of the Duke of Serra-Falco and heard a tale about the young madman who haunted them, the events of the novel are pure opera. Of course the nature of the *feuilleton* or newspaper serial demanded something at some distance from reality, but the fact that Mercier had recently been the opera critic of the New Orleans *Picayune* must also have contributed its share. The story lends itself effortlessly to an imaginary opera staging, with such standards of the lyric theater as a band of street Gypsies (*Mignon,* 1866), a masked costume ball (*Ballo in Maschera,* 1859), and a death-scene in a marble tomb (*Roméo et Juliette,* 1867) and a chance for a first-rate audience-stopper in the singing duel between the diva and the gypsy-girl. Indeed, though this is the purest guess work, one may readily believe that Mercier at first intended his work as a libretto for the lyric stage.

The plot begins with a Polish count who has reared his legitimate and bastard daughters together until the Gypsy mother of the latter stole her young child back to live with her tribe. Years have passed, and the Count travels about Europe with the remaining daughter, who is tubercular, but finds no help for her illness. She dies in Palermo, and he entombs her in a magnificent temple of marble where she reposes on a couch of sculpted stone. The Count then returns to Poland, whence the Czar soon ships him off permanently to Siberia. Meanwhile, the Gypsies rear their little charge carefully, for it is their intention to secure a magnificent sum from her father as ransom, if only they can find him. For years they follow him about Europe, always a little too late, and eventually appear in

Palermo some time after Manizka's death and the Count's ill-timed return to his homeland. It chances that the Gypsies, who wish to keep their domicile hidden because some of their activities are outside the law, have taken temporary quarters in the very cemetery where the nobleman had built his daughter's mausoleum. Forcing locks, they assign various tombs to members of the tribe. Fate sees to it that Manizka's resting place, cleared of course of its late occupant, is given to her Gypsy sister, whose memories of her former life are stirred up by the familiar name inscribed on her couch. Meanwhile, as she dances in the streets, the girl sees, and at first sight falls in love with, the recently returned Palermitan cello virtuoso Agniolo Calamatti, a sensitive, inexperienced musician returned from great successes in Paris. Agniolo is much in favor with the fun-loving Duke Serra di Falco, who arranges an entertainment at which all are to come in costume, but the ladies, who alone are to be masked, will reverse the usual procedure and invite the gentlemen to dance.

All Palermo talks of this festival, and the young Gypsy, though uninvited, attends the ball dressed gorgeously as an odalisque. Since it is hers to take the initiative, she spends much time with the young musician, who has early in the evening favored the company with one of his own compositions, drawn from a haunting air sung by the street Gypsies of the city. He in turn is much enamored of the mysterious odalisque. When, as another part of the evening's entertainment, a highly esteemed, young and charming operatic soprano of local origins is invited to sing, and the youth, who lives for music, seems swept away by the beauty of her singing, the odalisque proposes to please him further by following with the gypsy street song, to be accompanied by the cellist himself. To the immense surprise of all, her voice far outshines the professional's, who generously acknowledges as much, and inquires the odalisque's secret. She replies that to sing as she does one must first love as much.

As the festivities come to an end, she promises to meet with the young musician the next day, when she will reveal all to the one who is already madly in love with her. But he makes the mistake of following her that night to the vicinity of the abandoned cemetery where he sees her accosted by the rough Gypsy who has been her street partner. He observes her enter the cemetery, follows her, and a love scene follows, interrupted by her Gypsy dance-partner, who accuses her of having betrayed him and stabs her in the heart. When the musician had first asked her name, she gave him that of her dead sister, inscribed on the tomb. Thus the shock of her death is even greater for him when he realizes that the marble couch on which he lays her body is already marked, "Manizka, died at twenty." Clutching the dead body within the mausoleum, the musician is discovered by the police and a doctor, who charitably closes the bronze doors on Angiolo and his beloved, saying to the now-assembled throng, "I pray you, retire from this nuptial chamber." Angiolo now believes that it was death with which he exchanged his promises of love, and waits ardently for the return of his beloved and the transformation it will bring. Meanwhile, he haunts the gardens of the palace where they spent the one brief moment together.

Lidia

This is a light-hearted novel, at least for Mercier, and draws from his experience as a student in Paris. It is set in 1864 or 1865, only eight or nine years before it first appeared (1873) in the pages of the same New Orleans weekly paper which had just published Le Fou. Its comparatively low key is markedly different from that of its predecessor; Alcée Fortier called it an idyl, and one sees what he was driving at. The solitude of the chief male figure, the virtue of the protagonists, the setting in a green and park-like Parisian backwater, all help justify such a choice of terms. We know from the beginning that journeys will end in lovers meeting. Mercier, one may note, always managed to achieve a bridge with his Louisiana reader when the action was set in Europe. In Le Fou, Mercier himself is the narrator who in turn hears the story of the Palermitan madman. In Lidia the hermit-like student who lives high up among the leafy streets behind the Luxembourg is identified as a French colonial from Trinidad, but his name is Aurélien, and in Latin New Orleans is Neo-Aurelia. The character and situation are in some measure based on those of Mercier himself. In the short story "Emile des Ormiers" the Parisian student is a Martiniquais, and Théotime in *La Fille du Prêtre* is a native of Louisiana. The last two novels have Louisiana settings.

In *Lidia,* suspense is slight; we know from the outset that old Bellerive, who is practically a father to the anchoritic young scholar, is also an esteemed friend of Lidia's mother. This Bellerive had every intention of fostering a match between the two young people even if fate had not taken a hand and introduced them without his aid.

The complications begin when the wealthy old man, who is in Sicily on the aristocratic widow's business (for Lidia's father was a Sicilian), summons the widow to the island for certain transactions which require her presence and signature. Even though her lovely and intelligent daughter is over twenty-one, and so accomplished a singer that the family friend Giacomo Meyerbeer wants to have her create the role of Inès in his new opera *L'Africaine,* the widow decides to economize by placing her in a Parisian convent while she is to be away for six weeks. The mother superior is an old school acquaintance, Mother Bathilde. By chance, the convent garden is located very near Aurélien's top-floor apartment. Bathilde, one immediately discovers, is a somewhat sadistic prude who forbids all music, drives the birds away from the garden and views the presence of Lidia's caged lovebirds as a scandal and obscenity. Though he does provide the reader with a counterweight in the blunt, optimistic lower-class Sister Brigitte, who does good in the world by looking after the sick poor of the quarter, Mercier's anti-clerical bias leads him in some succeeding events nearly to the extremes of such anti-Catholic American propaganda as the much-circulated tale of Maria Monk in the convent.

It happens that both the Parisian convent's garden and Aurélien's apartment adjoin a handsome villa owned by a sculptor. Because she has talked to the sculptor's children through the fence, Lidia knows that the house is about to become vacant for the summer, and that there is an excellent piano in the salon. The chief privation of her enforced stay is the absence of music, and when the sculptor's family leave, she imprudently determines to steal in by night to use the instrument. Of course Aurélien overhears the music and, knowing the villa is empty, gets the keys from his own concierge, who has been left in charge. He tells her that he has heard strange music coming from the house and believes it to be occupied by a sorceress or a ghost, ideas which much impress the superstitious old woman.

The next time Lidia steals out to play the piano, he is already in concealment to observe her. Since she talks to herself, he learns that her birthday is at hand and that she will visit the salon on that occasion, but he does not learn her family name. The hitherto restrained and timid young man is now embarked on a wholly romantic line of conduct. He intends to reveal himself that birthday evening in the villa, accompanied by the proper kind of bouquet (knowledge gleaned from Lidia's soliloquies) and with the manuscript of a song he has written and had set by his acquaintance, the famous opera composer Meyerbeer! The youth is still inflamed by the memory of seeing her in négligé. And, rather daringly for Mercier, he had seen more of the chaste young woman than one ought to see of a Victorian virgin. On the appointed night he emerges from his concealment, a little like Madeline's lover in "The Eve of St. Agnes," and discovers that she has fallen instantly in love with him. They have hardly had time to elaborate on their sentiments, however, when the forces of evil intrude in the persons of Mother Bathilde, who has been increasingly aware of the little escapades over the wall, and her confessor, the youngish, well-built and despicable Jesuit, Père Espiou. With obvious pleasure they put the worst construction on the convent girl's presence in a deserted house in the arms of an unknown young man. Lidia returns to the convent, followed by the clerical brigade, and the next morning is told that she will be sent to another convent, where girls who have been guilty of indiscretions are kept under strict arrest. When so informed she refuses, and threatens to ward off the physical compulsions of Espiou with a little knife she keeps about her— Sicilian blood will tell. Finally, however she ceases to resist, and a cab appears in which Espiou is to escort her to the convent-prison. But all this physical contact and knife-drawing has aroused the ox-like Espiou, who, perhaps reasoning that she is free with her favors, makes her the most direct overtures. At that moment the cab is passing through one of the most savagely anti-clerical working-class quarters of Paris. Lidia throws open the curtains and threatens to raise the streets against her assailant. To avoid this, he allows her to escape, but gives out that she has fled to Italy to rejoin her mother. In fact, Lidia has gone to the house of her beloved god-mother, who gladly hears her whole story and volunteers not only to keep her until her mother's return, but to give all the assistance she can in finding the mysterious unknown lover.

Inconsequential as Espiou's misrepresentation might seem, it misleads Aurélien as to the whereabouts of his beloved and sends him desperately to Sicily, where, going from town to town and castle to castle, asking after a beautiful woman known only as Lidia, he eventually encounters the ancestral hall and gets information of Lidia's name and Paris address.

Meanwhile, despairing of ever finding Aurélien, Lidia falls gravely ill of typhoid fever, goes blind for a time and loses her lovely hair. It is her love of music which aids her recovery. As one might have guessed, Meyerbeer becomes the key to their reunion when he calls upon the widow Castrovillari and hears Lidia sing the love poem which he had set to music. Of course, he knows Aurélien well, as does old Bellerive, who is delighted to hear that his two young protégés have fallen in love, even under such unforeseen circumstances. Meanwhile, of course, Aurélien returns, and the lovers meet and immediately arrange a marriage that will give each of them sustenance and freedom in their respective arts, as well as the opportunity to bring up children with proper philosophic, religious and political sentiments.

As summarized thus, the story takes insufficient account of the well-drawn sketches of a number of men and women of the lower class who appear throughout the book: concierges, Napoleonic veterans, coachmen, inn-keepers, a café proprietor, Sicilian peasants, and the kindly little Soeur Brigitte from Toulouse. All challenge the givens of the typical stratified novelistic society of the nineteenth century by showing kindness, intelligence and virtue dominating over ignorance and coarseness in a nation moving away from aristocracy and into an era of the common man.

It is of course Mercier's hatred of monarchy and aristocracy that causes him to show so often his dislike of the established church of France, which was so firmly entrenched at this time against the republican and democratic desires of a large part of the populace. Such a split carried over, rather unnecessarily, into French Louisiana where, for instance, the Freemasons got control of the Board of Churchwardens of the St. Louis Cathedral during the 1840s and barred the Bishop from officiating in his own church. Though there could be no question of monarchic government or an established church in New Orleans, the hatreds which marked the French situation were duplicated in the new world. Mercier, who might have been more solicitous of getting a larger audience for himself, almost intentionally antagonized a majority of his potential public when he introduced a harsh prudish nun and an immoral Jesuit to a city where many young people were confided to the Ursulines and the Society of Jesus. In his remaining novels, Mercier continued to attack the proprieties of much of his audience. In case anyone had missed *Lidia,* the war against the Church would hardly be ignored by the Louisiana readers when four years later he scrutinized the question of sacerdotal celibacy in a novel bluntly entitled "The Priest's Daughter."

La Fille du Prêtre (The Priest's Daughter)

Quite different in bulk and in quality from *Le Fou* and *Lidia, La Fille du Prêtre* is a three-volume novel, nearly four hundred pages of small type. The central character is a Louisiana-born youth, Théotime de Kermarec, whose parents have returned to France. The parents are devout Catholics, but Théotime has a great-uncle who is a free-thinker. Long before the time of the action, he sat in the French Convention and condemned Louis XVI to the guillotine. The parents would like to see Théotime follow his elder brother in studying for the priesthood, but the great-uncle makes it clear that Théotime will be his heir only if he attends for a time a secular preparatory school. Thus the young man is sent to the Collège Louis-le-Grand, the distinguished "antechamber of the Sorbonne," which Mercier had himself attended. (These characters have vague prototypes in real Louisiana history. The regicide Lakanal taught for some years in New Orleans, and the Rouquette brothers, the elder of whom, Adrien, became a priest, were sent to church schools in Brittany. The Breton name Kermarec, of course, appears in the novel. Both Rouquette brothers had important careers in French literary Louisiana.) At Louis-le-Grand Théotime made several friends and absorbed certain philosophical and moral ideas which remained with him even after he returned to his seminary studies.

When time for his ordination approaches, he has grave doubts about his permanent commitment and seeks counsel from Ludovic, one of his school companions at Paris. In spite of his doubts, however, his parents' expectations and the insistence of church dignitaries that his intellect and gifts are needed by Holy Mother Church in its struggle against the freethinkers cause him to accept the priesthood. He is then sent for a time as curé to a village of southern Normandy, near a large factory, in fact, the very Usine de le Grande Montagne which Mercier served as doctor in 1859, a date close to the time of the novel. Obviously in a few years Mercier has traveled the distance from romanticism to realism, a change that took the French novel half a century to accomplish. Théotime is hardly settled in his country parsonage before the youthful drives of the blood begin to interfere with his priestly calling. He is full of desire for the charming young Jeanne, daughter of the village schoolmaster, and she is full of love for him. When she becomes pregnant, she tells him of her situation; he consults with his family, and he agrees to their counsel, that Jeanne should be offered a substantial dowry and married off to a farmer of the district.

A girl of good heart and some intelligence, Jeanne has believed in all his protestations and is desolated to discover what solution he offers. Her response is to leave home by night for Paris. There she finds out how hard it is for a woman to survive alone with any dignity, and for a while determines to throw herself into the Seine. When she has once made this decision, she writes a letter to Théotime, telling him of her intended suicide. She is dissuaded from this course of action at the last moment when she feels the child stirring in her womb for the first time. She then finds employment in the Dickensian household of a government clerk whose whole interest in life centers on his vegetable garden. The clerk's wife is an amazon who spends her days in violent loud quarrels with the three grown sons. Jeanne is given heavy work to do which would have been taxing even if she had not been pregnant; fortunately she attracts the attention of a young printer and his wife who live in the adjacent building, and they help her in the most arduous of her physical tasks. The wife Louise is also pregnant, and seeks medical counsel from a childhood friend of her husband who is now a doctor in a large free hospital. This is the same Ludovic who was Théotime's school-friend at Louis-le-Grand. Louise convinces Jeanne that she should seek help from Ludovic, and Ludovic falls in love with her during her confinement. She responds to his love, but falls victim to puerperal fever after bearing a girl-child who looks just like her mother. Little Jeannette is to be cared for by Louise but adopted by Ludovic, who with her will keep her mother's memory bright.

Meanwhile, Théotime can no longer bear the guilt he feels at having driven Jeanne to despair. Since she had sent him a letter announcing her later altered intention to commit suicide, he believes her dead, and suffers greatly from the falseness of his public position. When by chance an old school friend just demobilized from the Algerian campaigns stops overnight to call on the curé and talks incessantly about the forthcoming expedition of Garibaldi to free Sicily from the Bourbon yoke, Théotime's whole sociopolitical and religious outlook changes. As a result of this metanoia, he too steals off in the night; donning his old companion's zouave uniform he sets out for Italy. The time is 1860, and the former priest fights nobly for the liberty of Mercier's favorite island. In the battle which ensures the campaign's success, he falls wounded, struck in the chest by a Bourbon bullet. But after Naples surrenders it is not long before he is well enough to continue his struggle for human liberty by joining the Poles in their abortive revolt against the Czar in 1863. When this uprising fails, he is taken prisoner and sentenced to Siberia. The three books of this long novel are called respectively, "The Wrong Track," "Expiation," and "Rehabilitation." The acceptance of ordination and the rejection of fatherhood doubtless are the wrong track in question. The wound in Sicily and the exile in Siberia constitute the expiation.

Théotime's rehabilitation begins when he makes his way back to France. The date is now 1871. He offers his military experience to the new and fragile Third French Republic, just emerging after Louis Napoleon's débacle at Sédan and subsequent departure from Paris, forced by the insurrection of the Parisian National Guard and the setting up of the rival Commune. The moderate government of Louis Thiers has fled to Versailles, where Théotime joins the siege army that will invest Paris and subject the citizens to great privation and suffering before they assault it successfully. Historical account relates the hunger and destructive deeds of the communards, who murdered the Archbishop of Paris, and burned the Tuileries and the Hôtel de Ville.

It will be remembered that Ludovic and his foster-child inhabit Paris. Since Mercier, at least as novelist, believes in or utilizes some sort of beneficent fate, Théotime encounters them and saves them from death. Building-to-building fighting brings the Versailles forces to a cemetery, where strong resistance is offered. Here Jeanne lies buried, and here Ludovic and Jeannette have come in piety, only to be caught in the cross-fire. A general recognition and acknowledgement soon occurs, but much more time passes before Jeannette is brought back from New Caledonia, where she has gone with the deported "communards" to become the wife of the faithful Ludovic, who loves this reincarnation of the first Jeanne and marries her with her acknowledged father's consent. The complete rehabilitation is to be brought about by the establishment of a rustic, virtuous, deistic, secular school and orphanage to which the medical skills of Ludovic, the womanly love of Jeannette, and the intellectual and managerial gifts of the former priest can all be offered.

Mild as all this may seem today, we are told that at least two New Orleans newspapers, the *Abeille* and the *Picayune*, declined to review it because the subject was not thought fit for family newspapers. One can see why the *Abeille* would have hesitated, since so many of its readers were Catholic, but one must attribute the *Picayune's* reluctance to a Mother Bathilde-like prudery of the sort

that put lady authors on separate shelves, placed skirts on piano
legs and ordained separate cages for parakeets.

In issuing *La Fille du Prêtre,* Mercier carefully avoided the word
"roman" which carried implications of frivolity. Rather he entitled
it a "récit social," a social narrative. This change is in keeping
with the development French literature had been going through at
least since *Madame Bovary,* which twenty years before had caused
Flaubert to have to defend himself in court against charges of
immorality. With these changes *Le Fou* was wholly out of step,
while *Lidia* sought somewhat mechanically to combine the traditional material of a "roman" with sociological and political
didactism. At last in this novel he attempts to embody in his narrative the major social and moral concerns of the time as he saw them.
Perhaps Mercier erred in diagnosing sacerdotal celibacy as such a
problem, or even as a symbol for it; certainly for him it was a part of
the misdirected and self-seeking falseness he detected in the re-
actionary royalist/imperialist parties of France. The author believed that Théotime did the proper thing in abandoning the priesthood after finding himself so early to have betrayed its cardinal
rules. He would have an obligation, Mercier believed, to risk his
life in the pursuit of freedom, then of social order. He would have
believed such a man in real life further obliged to work diligently
for the people's moral and physical good in some task like
Théotime's colony for orphans. If some of his aims and beliefs seem
dated a century and more after publication, the polarities of his
time having been replaced by others which he could not have
dreamed of, we must not be too surprised. Mercier himself might
well be startled to find the church he so disliked still functioning,
though torn both by those who insist on priestly marriage and those
who demand the ordination of women. We must credit him with a
genuine if somewhat acrimonious sincerity, for he surely saw that
such a topic and position would lose him patients and friends in
literary life. More important than his sincerity, though, is his creation of a genuinely interesting, well told, well paced story, which is
at its most arresting when it forgets about the church question
(which is most of the time) and shows us the manners and mores of
contemporary life in France.

L'Habitation Saint-Ybars
ou Maîtres et Esclaves en Louisiane
(Saint-Ybars Plantation or Masters and Slaves in Louisiana)

Finally, just one hundred years ago, contemporary literary theory combined with a sense of alienation from the French scene (he had been reestablished for fully fifteen years in Louisiana) to make Mercier cultivate his own garden. The result was his most interesting and significant novel, though technically its predecessor surpasses it by far. Once again, as in *La Fille du Prêtre*, he subtitles his work a social narrative, but the society to be scrutinized is the French plantation caste of South Louisiana from which he had sprung. As compared with *La Fille* or even *Lidia*, in this Louisiana story Mercier makes considerable use of the devices of *feuilleton* and melodrama. Some of its material could have been written for a modern melodrama such as "Dallas." Besides the usual number of suicides and death scenes, in the course of the action we encounter a hurricane, an attempt at rape, a rescue on the Mississippi river, a foundling left on the doorstep, a duel, and other sensational incidents. But the work does not lack serious or lasting value, for with the traditional sensational material there appears both a detailed knowledge of life on a plantation and a wish to speak to the Louisianian's moral sense. In the latter regard, Mercier suggests the corrupting influence of slavery on the former owners and the contemporary need for white and black Louisianians to make common cause after the chaos of Reconstruction for the good of the state and of both races. Though his radical republicanism may have led him to decry old Louisiana institutions, he was far from hostile toward his fellow Louisianians, and he was strongly dedicated to keeping their French language alive. It was Mercier who conceived the plan of the *Athénée Louisianais* as a little academy, a rallying point for French writers and speakers and a force for encouraging the language among the young by means of medals and competitions. Influenced though he had been by the radicals of the

Second Republic, he had been more than willing in 1863 to advance the cause of the Southern Confederacy in *Du Panlatinisme,* which sought help from France, he argued rather speciously, the Southern victory would assist the survival of French in the new world. Perhaps in his scale of values it was more important to keep his homeland French than to free the slaves. But certainly when *Saint-Ybars* appeared eighteen years later, he had made up his mind: slavery was an evil.

The public expected Mercier's work to be offensive and scandalous. Most people just did not read the novel. But when the irenic Alcée Fortier touches on it a decade later in *Louisiana Studies,* he crawfishes about, praising the book not for its literary achievement but for its philological contributions in representing Antillean Creole. Cautiously he skirts the real issue, saying that the book ought to be put into English, for it is "a much more correct picture of Louisiana life than is to be found in many other works better known outside the state" (p. 62). Doubtless he had in mind Harriet Beecher Stowe and G.W. Cable. Fortier had indeed been Mercier's collaborator, but yet was a sincere Catholic conservative in a university then dominated by Presbyterian Confederate veterans. Neither his beliefs nor his prudence urged too frank a discussion of Mercier's views, especially in the light of the novelist's recent death. Somewhat later, when two disciples of Fortier address themselves briefly to the book, neither seems to have read it, but rather to assume from the master's ambiguities that the book is a defense of the *ancien régime.* I refer to the sketch of Louisiana literature by Edouard Fortier, Alcée's son, written while he taught at Columbia (*Les lettres françaises en Louisiane,* Quebec, 1915, pp. 15 ff.) and to the article on Mercier in the *Dictionary of American Biography* by Lionel Durel, who succeeded Fortier on the Tulane faculty and Mercier as secretary of the Athénée. Only in 1954 does Auguste Viatte in his *Histoire littéraire de l'Amerique française* express for the first time in print Mercier's real criticism of slavery in Louisiana (p. 289).

We first encounter M. de St.-Ybars, a very proper and prosperous up-river plantation owner, in the French Quarter of New Orleans, where he has come to hire a new tutor for his recalcitrant youngest son and to buy a new blacksmith for the "habitation." For the latter purpose he visits the slave emporium of the coarse and offensive Stovall, who makes a great contrast with the suave and aristocratic Creole. Rather unaccountably, the plantation owner is accompanied by his adolescent daughter "Chant d'Oisel." He has found the blacksmith he required, but in addition, his daughter has discovered a very light-skinned young slave girl named Titia who manages to communicate her terror: she is about to be purchased by two unsavory men who will doubtless then abuse her. Chant d'Oisel understands well enough and begs her indulgent father to give her the girl as a birthday gift. Reluctant at first, St.-Ybars consents, even though he learns that as part of the package he is also buying an elderly crippled dwarf, Titia's grandmother. She is soon nicknamed "Lagniappe" because she was thrown into the bargain. St.-Ybars discovers that the old woman has been well educated by her former master, whom she served as a secretary. This grotesque speaks excellent French and carries about her a duodecimo edition of Seneca. She now lives only for the happiness of Titia and for the child she carries—for Titia has been sold because of her love-affair with the former owner's son and heir.

St.-Ybars, who thus far seems to represent the idealized stereotype of every Creole's pre-war grandfather, elegant, courteous and rich, but haughty with those for whom he lacks respect, has to "purchase" a tutor for his son. The time is 1851. Antony Pelasge, who fought for the republican side in the revolution of 1848 while a student in Paris and was exiled to North Africa, has escaped to Spain and contrived to take passage for New Orleans. He has landed at the Esplanade dock that very day and by chance has witnessed St.-Ybars' slave transactions. Pelasge carries letters for the respected editor of one of the chief newspapers, and it is there that the planter who has come to seek out candidates encounters the émigré, who is seeking employment as a teacher in his new country. They rapidly strike a bargain, and he joins the growing train of people returning to St.-Ybars Plantation. Through Pelasge's eyes we shall perceive the events of the succeeding years. Indeed, he, Chant d'Oisel, and her twin brother Edmond, nicknamed

"Démon," whose education he supervises, are the only important characters who carry over into the second part of the novel, which describes events of the Reconstruction era. Pelasge is drawn as one of those philosophic radicals whom Mercier mingled with thirty years earlier and with whom he had already indicated much sympathy. A graduate of the Ecole Normale Superieure, Pelasge is admirably suited to the position which calls for changing the anti-academic attitudes of Edmond, formerly rebellious against all instruction. Edmond preferred the rough outdoor life to the acid ministrations and domineering ways of MacNara, an Irish ex-seminarian educated at Quebec. MacNara, a rather ridiculous figure, still remains in the neighborhood as a friend and admirer of the hard old Pulcherie, St.-Ybars' cousin who assists in the management of the "big house." This couple represent Mercier's continuing anti-clerical propaganda.

The elegant ancestral mansion is also inhabited by Mme. de St.-Ybars, a meek, browbeaten, nervous lady whose husband shows her little love or respect, though she has borne him numerous children. Their relationship is still deteriorating, in large measure because St.-Ybars is enamored of his daughter's governess and music teacher, the charming refugee from the Czar, Mlle. Nogolka, whose lovely young face contrasts startlingly with her white hair. Nogolka virtuously resists her employer and develops a love for Pelasge. Though a good number of the older St.-Ybars children inhabit the family mansion, they remain very shadowy figures throughout.

A major character, however, is "Vieumaite" or "Ole Massa," St.-Ybars' retiring, scholarly father, who shows symbolic physical evidence of the split nature of the old regime. Old St.-Ybars' face is totally asymetric. One side suggests a cruel severity, the other, which tends to dominate, a benevolent charm. This *philosophe* of the eighteenth-century school has long since turned over the management of his holdings to his son and consecrated himself to solitude and study of science and the classics in his little house and observatory. It is generally known, however, that in earlier days he had had a liaison with Semiramis, the free mulatto who still rules over all the female slaves of the plantation like an oriental queen, striking whom she will with the rod or "baleine" she always carries. To him she had borne Salvador, the symbolically named plantation carpenter, far more rational and benevolent than his legitimate half-brother, and marked by generosity and restraint.

Two other important house servants inhabit the big house. "Mamrie," who suckled the St.-Ybars twins and remains their mother's personal servant, is characterized by total devotion and fierce, savage dedication to those she loves. Lauzun, the young and dandyish valet of Monsieur, is allowed all sorts of self-indulgences and familiarities because he is the by-blow of St. Ybars' eldest son, and thus the master's first grandchild. Among the perquisites of Lauzun's office is a half-acknowledged *droit de seigneur* among the slave women of the plantation. It does not take him long to lust after the beautiful Titia, who, on the other hand, is still in love with the young white man who fathered her unborn child. Old Lagniappe, realizing that the child may well bear no trace of its black ancestry, has laid plans for it. She dickers with a wandering band of Choctaws until they agree to let the granddaughter run away with them and bear her child in their midst. (Obviously, an opera-lover like Mercier must find his Gypsy-surrogates where he can).

Pelasge's special charge "Démon" proves easy to redirect by a mixture of common sense and Rousseauistic pedagogy. The boy's instruction is begun without his knowing it, in such tasks as explaining the intricacies of the plantation and its surroundings to Pelasge. He is set to conducting a truck-farm for profit, and succeeds admirably. All this establishes a rapport between the two which will last until Edmond's death. The boy thrives and gives promise of an excellent future. Pelasge, finding that he and "Vieumaite" are also mutually sympathetic, is constantly invited to visit the old man in his study where they read the last shipment of books from France and discuss abstract questions.

Everyone recognizes that the relations of St.-Ybars and his wife have steadily worsened. More and more of the practical affairs of the household the husband confides to his severe and unfeeling Cousin Pulchérie, while he treats his wife with ill-concealed contempt, even before the servants. His passion for Nogolka is at last shockingly revealed late one night, when Pelasge, returning from a visit with "Vieumaite," overhears St.-Ybars' clandestine meeting with the unwilling music teacher beneath the great old oak which also shades the tombs of early St.-Ybars. When Nogolka refuses to become his kept woman, he attempts to rape her on the graves of his ancestors. Pelasge does not intervene, however, for her resistance and the advent of a severe electrical storm, precursor to the next day's hurricane, serve to postpone the master's ardors.

The rape and the hurricane are not the only remarkable events of these Aristotelian twenty-four hours. Hardly have St.-Ybars, Nogoïka and Pelasge retired in several directions before a shadowy figure ascends the gallery of the mansion and deposits before the main door a carefully wrapped golden-haired blue-eyed girl-child. The reader, of course, will guess the identity of the child and thus anticipate the tragic complications of the second half of the novel. Several members of the family are charmed with the little one, and she is taken into the household. Chant d'Oisel and Edmond become her godparents, and a reasonable but incorrect guess is made as to her origins. No one suspects that she may not be Caucasian. Thus enters the theme of the "passé-blanc," used so effectively by George Washington Cable in *Madame Delphine*, which is almost exactly contemporaneous. The discovery of the baby does not for long allay the frustrated anger St.-Ybars feels over the events of the night before. His poor wife responds with an agitated nervousness, so that she spills a bowl of the soup she has been serving at the midday meal. Her husband "chided her in words, harsh at first, that became progressively coarser and even insulting." A silence falls over the table until young Edmond, his fists clenched, his face afire, strikes the table and cries out, 'No! I won't stand for it! It isn't fair.'" These words cause his father to lay hold of the whip used to discipline the slaves and order "Démon" to his knees. The boy refusing, the father strikes him at the base of the neck. When Pelasge intervenes, he is himself threatened with the whip, whereupon Nogolka throws herself between the two to protect the one she loves, but is struck on the head, so that the blood flows, staining her white hair red. Predictably, St.-Ybars blames his son for the harm he has done his would-be mistress and again assaults the boy, but is stopped for a time by his daughter, who wrenches the "baleine" from his grasp after "Démon" has taken several blows to the face. The scene marks a striking contrast to the courtly St.-Ybars the reader first encountered.

The faithful "Mamrie," hearing that Edmond is being beaten, grasps a nearby wood-chopper's hatchet and threatens her master. He strikes Edmond again and she throws the weapon at his head, but it passes through the window and buries itself in a magnolia tree. She has committed a capital offense. Taking advantage of his father's stunned surprise, the boy runs off and Mamrie is placed in the plantation lock-up to await the master's judgment. Soon word comes that "Démon," who has tried to cross the river to seek refuge among some relatives, has lost control of his skiff in the mounting winds. Still afloat, he is in grave danger. Suddenly St.-Ybars cries out, "My child is lost, and it is my own fault; it is God's vengeance on me!"

Salvador, St.-Ybars' half-brother, quickly organizes a rescue team which includes St.-Ybars himself. Edmond is rescued, and St.-Ybars nearly drowns in the rescue attempt. He thus shows his better side in deeds, much as his father was often dominated by the benevolent half of his physiognomy.

At the time St.-Ybars despaired of Edmond's safety, Salvador had chided him for believing that God could punish a sinful father by killing an innocent child. Significantly, the name Salvador (Savior), his carpenter's trade, and the contrast with his mother, whose name suggests the pre-Christian cruelties of Assyria, all imply the mixed-blood Creoles may hold the key to salvation in the post-Civil War era of Louisiana.

Later, when Mamrie is condemned to the lesser domestic punishment of a public flagellation, Edmond conceals himself in the upper reaches of the "big house" and lets the Negroes all know that the first one who strikes his old wet-nurse will be shot. All are naturally reluctant, and the white overseer has to take over the task. He too would have lost his life had Nogolka not determined to use her interest with St.-Ybars to crave a pardon for the slave-woman. This St.-Ybars grants, but furiously, and grasping his shotgun, strides away. Sémiramis, speaking for the "old law," is heard to say,

"Whites don't know how to rule nowadays. Ten mo' years and there be no mo' slavery."

After such events, it is evident that Nogolka must leave the plantation. Pelasge also makes it clear to St.-Ybars that "Démon" has suffered too great a blow to his pride to remain for long, and must be sent away to Paris for further schooling. Before Nogolka leaves, she tells Pelasge of her secret admiration, and he in turn confides that he is in love with Chant d'Oisel St.-Ybars.

Two incidents remain in the crowded ante-bellum portion of Mercier's plantation history. First, the evil valet Lauzun is determined to have the body of young Titia, who had returned quietly from her Indian sojourn some time after her baby appeared on the doorstep. He has waylaid old Lagniappe, nearly blinded her, and stolen from her a paper which reveals the true antecedents of the golden-haired child whom the St.-Ybars, by some sort of cosmic irony, have named "Blanchette." Faced with the alternatives of yielding her child or seeing her a slave, Titia drowns herself in the plantation well, after she has solemnly threatened the superstitious Lauzun that she will haunt him forever if he breathes one word of her child's origin.

Second, old St.-Ybars gives a prophetic death-bed speech in which he foresees all the misfortunes of the imminent Civil War. When "Vieumaite" dies, he leaves his retreat to Pelasge, who must use it to sustain the family in the event that disaster besets the St.-Ybars.

Wisely, Mercier skirts the events of the Civil War entirely and devotes the second, shorter part of his book to the racial problem in the post-war era. The war, though undescribed, has changed the plantation and its people. St.-Ybars and several of his sons have died in battle, the other children are dispersed in Texas or California, the plantation house is in ruins, and all cultivation has ceased. Pulchérie has started a boarding house for Federal officers in New Orleans, and has as her star-boarder MacNara, now prominently involved in Republican politics. Equally prominent in the carpet-bag government is the miserable Lauzun. Near the ruined plantation, living in Vieumaite's house, are the mentally failing Mme.

St.-Ybars, Chant d'Oisel, the foundling Blanchette, and Pelasge. Edmond, too young for the war, is still studying in Paris. He has not returned since the war, and hardly knows the privations the rest have incurred in order that he might continue his studies. Toward the end, they are able to send him his remittance only because "Mamrie," free but still faithful, goes to New Orleans and becomes a praline vendor on Canal Street, earning the pittance required.

There has been no real opportunity for the love affair between Pelasge and Chant d'Oisel to develop. The hardships and deaths with which she has been surrounded and the privations of her impoverished life have a bad effect. Eventually, she consents to a death-bed wedding, a lugubrious bit of sentimentalism rendered unrealistic and a little absurd by the presence of a justice of the peace, rather than a priest, a substitution no nineteenth century Creole lady would have dreamed of consenting to. No sooner is the civil knot tied but death comes for the lovely Chant d'Oisel, and Pelasge is left with a terrible sense of loss and a feeling that all life is vanity. He remains with the old lady and Blanchette and greets Edmond when he finally returns from Paris.

Together he and Pelasge visit the plantation's ruins and converse about the future of the state. Pelasge, who is Mercier's "raison-neur," waxes philosophic. He insists that both the Northern Republicans and blacks who would destroy the old ruling class and the plantation whites are wrong. The first would exterminate the whites. The second would starve off the blacks by bringing in European or Oriental labor to work their spreads. Neither course will work; the only true solution is to be found in an acceptance of the new freedom and rights of the blacks, who must be educated in reading, writing, and morality, while they in turn accept the universal need of mankind to work and to rise by one's own efforts. If they can do so, the blacks will prove the key to a prosperity even greater than that which existed before the War. Only the memories of years of suffering and death keep the whites ignorant and proud, and thus unable to perceive that the blacks of Louisiana are not really their enemies but their natural allies.

Inevitably, Edmond falls in love with his godchild Blanchette. Lauzun tells the cruel Pulcherie the secret of Blanchette's birth;

the passing years and his rise in the world have freed him from fears of retribution by the spirit of Titia. Soon the whole district is whispering about Blanchette's mixed blood and Edmond is forced into a duel with a well-known neighborhood fire-eater who has insulted her in his presence. He kills the man on the field of honor, but soon realizes that they are too poor to live except in Louisiana and that in Louisiana they can expect no decent life together. A fatalistic Blanchette ascribes their dilemma to a malevolent fate, but "Démon" replies, "Don't say that we are succumbing to the force of destiny! Fate has nothing to do with these events; the executioner who is separating us is the child of pride and ignorance; he has no existence in the world of nature, and no name in the eternal order of things. In the human language of this earth he is entitled *Prejudice*."

Meanwhile "Mamrie," who has gone blind, has learned from Lagniappe about this terrible blow to her granddaughter's happiness and thereby to the beloved "Démon." She vows to have her revenge on Lauzun. The train of events leads Edmond to suicide. He takes a large dose of strychnine, and is discovered, dying, by his beloved, who in turn seizes his pistol and shoots herself. Thus the lovers, crossed not by the stars but by convention, die together and are united like Romeo and Juliet in the tomb. They are buried together beneath the ancient oak which shades the graves of all the St.-Ybars: the old line is now extinct. But Mamrie has still to fulfill her vow; she puts an end to Lauzun and dies in the process. There remains nothing for Pelasge but to turn over his little holding to the intelligent blacks who have helped, and return to Europe. The Third Republic is dawning, and he will rejoin Nogolka, who has since married an elderly Slavic philosopher, part Marx and part Count Tolstoy. Together, they will all work for the slow improvement of mankind.

Surely Alcée Fortier was right when he said, only a few years after the book came out, that it should have been translated into English. Mercier had a penchant for minorities and losing causes. Louisiana's literate audience in French language can never have numbered more than a hundred thousand. By the 1880s this number was steadily diminishing; indeed, Mercier foresaw the extinc-

tion of French in his native state by 1950. But just as he had alien-
ated many of the diminishing band by his imprudent frankness and
his anticlericalism, he went on insisting on writing in French a
book which, had it come out on a national level, riding the crest of
G. W. Cable's popularity, would surely have attracted much attention and perhaps influenced the thought of the South and the nation.

Mercier had thirteen years yet to live when St.-Ybars appeared,
but after sixty-five he was not to accomplish anything as significant
as this "récit social," the ideas of which have gained general
acceptance in the deep South and effectively changed the social
structure only a full century after Mercier's book appeared. It de-
serves to be republished now.

Johnelle

Not until 1891, when Mercier was seventy-five and his powers
were flagging, did he finally set one of his novels in New Orleans.
Though its clinical attention to physical and psychological detail
may seem a direct imitation of the naturalistic theories of Zola, the
novel turns out to be a return to the fantastic and somewhat hysteri-
cal world of *Le Fou*. The subject is an artist's insanity. As in *Lidia*,
the chief male character is a reclusive artist and lover of music and
letters. Doubtless he derives a good deal from Mercier himself, but
his Italian origin is emphasized. Interestingly, one of the few Italian Creole families was renowned for the distinction of its members and for the recurring imbalance which attacked some of them.
Of some influence on Mercier's central character may have been
the novelist and painter Edward Dessommes, who when he returned to his native city was unable to follow any career for long,
and lived out the latter part of his life in rustic Mandeville. Edward
Dessommes may also be a real-life prototype for the doctor-suicide
in his brother George's naturalistic *Tante Cydette*. He had also
studied medicine in Paris, although something of Mercier is in that
portrait of the medical littérateur. *Cydette* had just come out when
Mercier began *Johnelle*.

Though this last novel's chief clinical subject is Tito Metelli's insanity, its chief propaganda is directed against abortion and infanticide. Mercier remained a "liberal"; he diagnosed these phenomena as deriving from the selfishness of those who could not be bothered with offspring and the false shame of those who were dominated by religious and conventional shame. He came out therefore very strongly for what today is called "the right to life."

Shortly before the Civil War, Metelli's prosperous father had married a "fast" and beautiful young New York girl who was devoid of love and wanted him entirely as a wealthy "catch." When the Civil War leaves him poor, she feels cheated and determines to have no children. She therefore has recourse to abortionists, who will even destroy the new-born child if their previous ministrations have not worked. All of Cordelia Metelli's devices have long been well-known to her mother-in-law. This fundamentally good woman hates her daughter-in-law, knowing that her son turned to drink and to suicide out of horror at his wife's courses. She knows even that Tito was born only because the abortionist failed Cordelia. But time has passed, and the young man has gone on to study art and architecture at Tulane. A natural solitary, he cultivates interests in music and literature in the attic apartment of an old double house on Bayou Road (now Gov. Nicholls St.) in the Faubourg Trémé. His crippled mother, constantly complaining, constantly critical, occupies the lower floor, and is waited on by a faithful black woman who once belonged to his father's family. The boy Tito had wanted a little sister, and has the most vivid memories of the birth of Johnelle, reported as still-born, but actually, as he later learns, has been pierced through the skull by the abortionist midwife. He sees her, laid out by the kind grandmother, but never diagnoses the red spot which he always sees on her forehead in his imagination.

Tito has an unhealthy preoccupation with this "dream sister" and utilizes his artistic skill to paint a succession of portraits, picturing the dead girl as she progresses through childhood and adolescence. He often imagines her presence and lets this company substitute for ordinary human intercourse. Almost without friends, he is saving for the day when he can afford a prolonged trip to France and his ancestral Italy.

But this journey is never to be, however, for one afternoon after a

torrential rain he overhears his grandmother, who has sought shelter from the same downpour, verbally attacking Cordelia with a
review of the abortions and infanticides already mentioned. The
double shock of knowing that he was not wanted by his mother and
that the red spot on Johnelle's forehead was a murderer's wound
sends him into brain fever. From that moment, Tito's fate is sealed.
He will live for a time, but more and more in a world of dreams,
painting more and more portraits of the dead sister and believing
that she really comes to visit him in his apartment.

Tito's next-door neighbor, a kindly "traiteuse" and midwife,
another of Mercier's Dickensian types, convinces the family that
they should call a certain Doctor Plana, a mysterious personage
recently arrived from Mexico, though of French education. This
doctor becomes Tito's constant companion for the rest of his short
life, determined to cure him even if by the most unorthodox
methods, but failing in the end. To Tito he reveals his own remarkable story: he was the child of an archbishop and an adulterous
marquise. They have never seen him, but his life and education
have been provided for, even the procuring of an excellent medical
practice in Mexico City for him when he graduates. There Plana is
forced into a duel with a loose-tongued Frenchman who has somehow learned Plana's antecedents. When he kills the gossiper, he is
forced to leave Mexico for New Orleans with his protégé, a pure-
-blooded Aztec eunuch *ex nativitate* whom he has rescued when
the parents exposed the abnormal child. Plana has taught himself
the horologist's trade, and he in turn has taught his ward. "Illud"
the eunuch and his clocks are perhaps allegorical, like several other
aspects of *Johnelle*, but they exemplify Mercier's gift for the
grotesque.

Plana's revelations to his patient come just before he has heartily
urged Tito, now that he is somewhat better, to undertake the plan-
ned trip to Europe, in the secret hope that this change of scene will
detach him from his delusions. The expectations of readers are
always based on the assumption that a character is introduced with
much detail only because such details affect his role in the principal intrigue. But here, not so. Just when we begin to look forward to
Plana's accompanying Tito to Europe, where the doctor's ambig-

uous past and its problems will somehow be resolved, Tito falls into a decline, and the whole project of the European trip is abandoned, though the ticket is already purchased.

It is as though Mercier had intended such an elaboration to fill the middle pages of the book, but somehow old age caught up with him, and his remaining energies could not cope with the plot as he had intended it. Rather, he hurried on to the denouement. As *Johnelle* was written, Tito's relapse is a point from which the novel hurries to its evident and inevitable end, the protagonist's death.

The last chapters are concerned with Plana's empiric scheme to shake Tito from his fantasy world. He has encountered a young woman in his practice whose family is very grateful to the doctor. They are therefore willing to allow him to employ this young girl, who closely resembles the portraits of the adolescent Johnelle, as a substitute for the dream-sister. Thus Tito Metelli will be lured back into the world of flesh and blood. Her visits to the Metelli house at first seem to work, but Tito finally makes it quite clear that although this young woman may indeed come from beyond the grave, she is assuredly not his sister. Shortly after Plana's failure, Tito, who has always taken solitary walks to the river, takes one last trip, and ends his life, as his father had before him. They find his panama hat on the wharf. Plana and his eunuch, much disturbed by his death, broach a bottle of ancient sherry and drink it to the memory of their friend. They then pack up their few belongings and leave New Orleans forever. The faithful former slave leaves Cordelia to her own devices, Tito is buried, and the novel ends.

Evidently, there is something wrong with this work. If fiction is to be successful it needs more interaction among the characters than occurs in *Johnelle*, unless the novelist is far more modern than Mercier and utilizes stream of consciousness or the "monologue intérieur." We are told that Tito is gifted, but we see no buildings, and as for art view only the morbid paintings of the dream-sister. He has no friends and no real enemies except his mother. His insanity may be close enough to clinical reality to interest alienists; it is not likely to grasp the common reader's imagination sufficiently to make it succeed as fiction. Had the trip to Europe been inserted, we might have seen more of Plana, who is much more interesting than his patient. Indeed, Mercier might well have done better to use Plana as his central figure. But this is to write of what might have been and not what is. On finishing *Johnelle* we are left with a feeling that we have been cheated. Despite the 221 page length, we sense that little has happened or been experienced, that we have met ideas but not people. Thus the pendulum has swung full arc from *Le Fou,* where we encountered sensations but not people. Passing through "social narrative," we have arrived at a genre where the plot and characters hardly count unless to illustrate a morbid mental condition or condemn an immoral social practice.

Both Mercier's short stories, "Emile des Ormiers" and "L'Anémique," deal with the sufferings of solitary and friendless young men with mental and physical problems. Emile commits suicide. In a Poe-like setting in Savannah the anemic central character of the other tale turns to procuring the deaths of children to sustain his increasing vampiric tendencies. These tales hardly equal the novels. One is another development in brief of the typical Mercier hero in the typical Mercier Parisian student scene. The other, more interesting, is his boldest attempt at developing his gift for the grotesque. Neither tale will make or break Mercier as a writer of fiction. Edgar Poe is not challenged.

The end of Alfred Mercier's career as novel writer had come. In less than three years' time he was to die a slow death from cancer and be buried from the house of his married daughter with all the rites of the church he had so strongly excoriated. One wonders whether the old man had some change of heart at the end, or more likely, whether a kindly priest eased his lady-parishioner's pain by providing a conventional end for her unconventional father.

Nearly fifty years before, Cyprien Dufour had written a series of journalistic sketches of the literary figures of New Orleans. He included Mercier for having published *Niagara* and the *Rose de Smyrne.* After quoting a bit, he concludes that Mercier's métier is not poetry but the prose of a man in the public arena. Far away, in France, Mercier may never have seen Dufour's remarks, but he came to a similar conclusion. For the last thirty years of his life he sought to lend his pen to all the causes he believed in, and we must honor him for his dedication and perseverence. That he achieved little is certain. His audience was minute, and half-alienated before it picked up the page. The one thing he did in his own time was prolong the use of literary French in Louisiana for the better part of a half-century, through the encouragement given by means of the *Athénée*. But in this day when ethnicity is respectable for the first time in America, are we not justified in looking back at his fictional corpus to reexamine his works and analyze them for their contributions to American literature and culture?

PRIMARY AND SECONDARY BIBLIOGRAPHY

Novels, Novellas and Short Stories of Alfred Mercier:

Hénoch Jédésias, otherwise *Auri-Fames ou l'Avare de New York*, Printed but not published, Paris, 1848. First published in *L'Epoque*, New Orleans, 1869; only a few installments survive. Republished in *Comptes-rendus de l'Athenée Louisianais*, 1892–93.

Le Fou de Palerme, first appeared serially in *Le Carillon* of New Orleans, 1873, then issued in same year as a book by *Le Carillon*. Neither form bears Mercier's name.

Lidia, first appeared serially in *Le Carillon*, late 1873; revised and again published serially in *Le Franco-Louisianais*, 1887. Published in book form, 1887, by Eugene Antoine's Imprimerie Franco-Americaine.

La Fille du Prêtre: Récit social, printed in three volumes, "Fausse Route" (1877), "Expiation" (1877) and "Rehabilitation" (1878), all by Imprimerie Cosmopolite of New Orleans.

L'Habitation Saint-Ybars, ou Matres et esclaves en Louisiane: Récit social. Published as a book by Eugene Antoine, Imprimerie Franco-Americaine, 1881.

"Emile des Ormiers," first appeared in *Franco-Louisianais*, 29 May 1886. Reprinted as a pamphlet, n.d., and (in copy I have seen) with the name of Alfred Mercier printed on a label at the end.

"L'Anémique," n.d., a pamphlet identical in type and format with the pamphlet version of "Emile des Ormiers." In the Louisiana State University copy it too is signed with the printed pasted label at the end.

Johnelle appeared in book form only; New Orleans; Eugene Antoine, 1891.

Selected Biographical, Bibliographical and Critical Writings:

D'Abzac, Vicomte Paul. "Excursions en Louisiane." New Orleans: Eugene Antoine's Imprimerie Franco-Americaine, 1882.

Dufour, Cyprien. *Esquisses locales par un inconnu.* New Orleans, 1847. Chapter xlvii, trans. Edna M. Barlow, *Louisiana Historical Quarterly,* 15 (April 1932), 280–81.

Durel, Lionel C. "Alfred Mercier" in the *Dictionary of American Biography, 12, p. 546.*

Fortier, Alcée. "Alfred Mercier" (a eulogy) printed in *Comptes-rendus,* 1 July 1894.

Fortier, Alcée. *Louisiana Studies.* New Orleans: Hansell, 1894, pp. 58–62.

Fortier, Alcée. *Louisiana.* Madison, Wisc.: Century Historical Association, 1914. Vol. IIJ, pp. 146–47.

Fortier, Edouard. "Les écrivains francais de la Louisiane" in *Memoires, Premier Congrès de la langue française au Canada.* Quebec: Presses Universitaires Laval, 1914.

Jones, John Maxwell, Jr. *Slavery and Race in Nineteenth-Century Louisiana French Literature.* n. p., printed by the author, 1978. This work came to the present author's attention after his article was submitted. It discusses *Le Fou* and *Johnelle,* and in its treatment of *St.-Ybars* anticipates the present study in one or two points.

Tinker, Edward Larocque. *Les Ecrits de langue française en Louisiane au XIX siecle.* Paris, H. Champion, 1932, pp. 351–64. The most important study and bibliography, but not always exact.

Viatte, Auguste, *Histoire littéraire de l'Amerique française des origines à 1950.* Quebec: Presses universitaires Laval, 1954, pp. 286–291 and *passim.* Necessarily superficial but also doctrinally antagonistic.

Nineteenth Century New Orleans in Books

COLEEN COLE SALLEY

For the following bibliography, four major sources for materials about the city and Louisiana were consulted: the extensive collections of the Historic New Orleans Collection (533 Royal, Florence Jumonville, Lbn.), the New Orleans Public Library (219 Loyola Ave., Cullen Hamer, Lbn.), and Tulane University (6823 St. Charles Ave., Jane Stevens, Lbn.). These collections are rich storehouses of original and facsimile letters, journals, diaries, and theses, in addition to books, in-print and out of print.

The fourth source is a book dealer who specializes in in-print publications about Louisiana and the Deep South: Library Sales and Service, Inc. (1458 North Broad Ave., Joe and Liz Bruns, owners). They represent approximately two hundred publishers, many of whom are one-time publishers (a church, a guild) of a local history. They supply in-print titles.

The caption "Lagniappe" was the concession of the special editor (a scholar) to the whims of the bibliographer (a generalist) when agreement about the significance of a publication could not be reached. Some of the titles are slight publications, restricted to a small area of the city and its history. Others perpetuate those legends about New Orleans which should be a part of folk literature. But therein lies the charm of New Orleans: everyone has a story to tell.

HISTORY AND BIOGRAPHY

The Purchase and Early Years of the Century:

Barbe-Marbois, Francois. *The History of Louisiana: Particularly of the Cession of That Colony to the United States of America.* Baton Rouge: Louisiana State Univ. Press, 1977.

Chidsey, Donald Barr. *Louisiana Purchase.* New York: Crown, 1972.

Claiborne, W.C.C. *Official Letter Books of W.C.C. Claiborne, 1801–1816.* 6 vols. Ed. Dunbar Rowland. Jackson, Miss.: State Department of Archives and History, 1917.

DeConde, Alexander. *This Affair of Louisiana: A New Interpretation of the American Purchase of Louisiana,* New York: Scribner's, 1976.

Freiberg, Edna B. *Bayou St. John: In Colonial Louisiana 1699–1803.* New Orleans: Author, 1980.
Hatfield, Joseph T. *William Claiborne: Jeffersonian Centurion in the American Southwest.* University of Southwestern Louisiana History Series. Lafayette: Univ. of Southwestern Louisiana, 1976.
Landry, Stuart Omer. *Sidelights on the Battle of New Orleans.* New Orleans: Pelican, 1965.
Lyon, E. Wilson. *The Man Who Sold Louisiana: The Career of Francois Barbe-Marbois.* Norman: Univ. of Oklahoma Press, 1974.
Pitot, James. *Observations on the Colony of Louisiana from 1796 to 1802.* Baton Rouge: Louisiana State Univ. Press, 1979.

War of 1812 and the Battle of New Orleans:

Brown, Wilbert S. *The Amphibious Campaign for West Florida and Louisiana, 1814–1815; a Critical Review of Strategy and Tactics at New Orleans.* Tuscaloosa: Univ. of Alabama Press, 1969.
Carter, Samuel. *Blaze of Glory; the Fight for New Orleans, 1814–1815.* New York: St. Martin's, 1971.
DeGrummond, Jane Lucas. *The Baratarians and the Battles of New Orleans.* Baton Rouge: Louisiana State Univ. Press, 1961.
Forrest, Charles Ramus. *The Battle of New Orleans: A British View.* New Orleans: Hauser Press, 1961.
Latour, Major, A. LaCarriere. *Historical Memoir of The War in West Florida and Louisiana in 1814–1815, with an Atlas.* 1816; rpt. Gainesville: Univ. of Florida Press, 1964.
Reilly, Robin. *The British at the Gates: The New Orleans Campaign in the War of 1812.* New York: Putnam, 1974.
Saxon, Lyle. *Lafitte the Pirate.* New Orleans: Robert L. Crager, 1930.

Civil War Years:

Brooks, Charles B. *The Siege of New Orleans.* Seattle: Univ. of Washington Press, 1961.
Capers, Gerald M. *Occupied City: New Orleans Under the Federals 1862–1865.* Lexington: Univ. of Kentucky, 1965.
Caskey, Willie. *Secession and Restoration of Louisiana.* 1938; rpt. New York: DaCapo Press, 1970.
Dufour, Charles. *The Night the War Was Lost.* Garden City, N. Y.: Doubleday, 1960. Battle of New Orleans, 1862.
Fisher, Roger. *The Segregation Struggle in Louisiana, 1862–1877.* Urbana: Univ. of Illinois Press, 1974.
Meade, Robert Douthat. *Judah P. Benjamin, Confederate Statesman.* New York: Oxford Univ. Press, 1943.
Reinders, Robert C. *End of an Era: New Orleans (1850–1960).* New Orleans: Pelican, 1964.
Taylor, Joe Gray. *Louisiana Reconstructed, 1863–1877.* Baton Rouge: Louisiana State Univ. Press, 1980.

Trefousse, Hans L. *Ben Butler: The South Called Him Beast!* New York: Octagon, 1974.

Williams, T. Harry. *P.G.T. Beauregard: Napoleon in Gray.* Baton Rouge: Louisiana State Univ. Press, 1955.

Willson, Backles. *John Slidell and the Confederates in Paris.* New York: AMS Press, 1932.

Winters, John. *Civil War in Louisiana.* Baton Rouge: Louisiana State Univ. Press, 1980.

The Last Century:

Chandler, David Leon. *Brothers in Blood: The Rise of the Criminal Brotherhoods.* New York: Dutton, 1975. Origin of the Mafia in Louisiana.

Gambins, Richard. *Vendetta.* New York: Doubleday, 1977. The assassination of David Hennessy, 32-year-old superintendent of the New Orleans Police, in 1890 led to the mass lynching of eleven Italian-Americans suspected of the crime.

Jackson, Joy. *New Orleans in the Gilded Age: Politics and Urban Progress, 1880–1886.* Baton Rouge: Louisiana State Univ. Press, 1969.

Landry, Stuart Omer. *The Battle of Liberty Place: The Overthrow of Carpetbag Rule in New Orleans-September 14, 1874.* New Orleans: Pelican, 1955.

General History:

Conrad, Glenn R., ed. *Readings in Louisiana History.* Baton Rouge: Louisiana Historical Association, 1978.

Davis, Edwin. *Story of Louisiana.* 4 vols. Baton Rouge: Claitor's, n.d. Three volumes are biographical dictionaries.

Dufour, Charles L. *Ten Flags in the Wind.* New York: Harper, 1976.

Fossier, Albert Emile. *New Orleans, the Glamour Period, 1800–1840; a History of the Conflicts of Nationalities, Religion, Morals, Cultures, Laws, Politics, and Economics during the Formative Period of New Orleans.* New Orleans: Pelican, 1957.

Gayarre, Charles. *History of Louisiana: Its First Half Century as an American State.* Vol. IV. New Orleans: Pelican, 1974.

Huber, Leonard V. *New Orleans: A Pictorial History.* New York: Crown, 1971. Earliest history to present with more than 1,000 illustrations.

Kendall, John Smith. *History of New Orleans.* 3 vols. Chicago: Lewis Publishing Co., 1922.

King, Edward. *Louisiana 100 Years Ago.* 2 vols. 1873; rpt. Albuquerque: Sun Publishers, 1976. New Orleans and environs in the mid-19th century, originally published by Scribners and profusely illustrated.

Lewis, Peirce F. *New Orleans—The Making of an Urban Landscape.* Cambridge, Mass.: Ballinger, 1976. Sociological and geographical history of the development of the insular city of New Orleans.

Black History and Culture:

Blassingame, John. *Black New Orleans 1860–1880*. Chicago: Univ. of Chicago, 1973.

Desdunes, Rudolphe Lucien. *Our People and Our History*. 1911: rpt. Baton Rouge: Louisiana State Univ. Press, 1973. The Creole people of color.

Haskins, James. *The Creoles of Color of New Orleans*. New York: Crowell, 1975.

MacDonald, Robert R. *Louisiana's Black Heritage*. New Orleans: Louisiana State Museum, 1979.

Ripley C. Peter. *Slaves and Freedmen in Civil War Louisiana*. Baton Rouge: Louisiana State Univ. Press, 1976.

Sterkx, H. E. *The Free Negro in Ante-Bellum Louisiana*. Rutherford, N. J.: Fairleigh Dickinson Univ. Press, 1972.

Taylor, Joe Gray. *Negro Slavery in Louisiana*. New York: Negro Universities Press, 1963.

DESCRIPTIONS, DAILY LIFE

Carter, Hodding.*Past as Prelude: New Orleans (1718–1968)*. New Orleans: Tulane Univ., 1968.

Castellanos, Henry C. *New Orleans As It Was: Episodes of Louisiana Life*. 1895; rpt. Baton Rouge: Louisiana State Univ. Press, 1979.

Didimus, H. *New Orleans As I Found It*. New York: Harper, 1845.

Federal Writers' Project of the Works Progress Administration for the City of New Orleans. *New Orleans City Guide*. Boston: Houghton, Mifflin, 1938.

Hall, A. Oakey. *Manhattaner in New Orleans, or: Phases of "Crescent City" Life*. 1851; rpt. Baton Rouge: Louisiana State Univ. Press, 1976.

New Orleans Press. *Historical Sketch Book and Guide to New Orleans and Environs*. New York: Will H. Coleman, 1885.

Norman, Benjamin Moore. *Norman's New Orleans and Environs*. 1845; rpt. Baton Rouge: Louisiana State Univ., 1976.

Saxon, Lyle. *Old Louisiana*. New York: D. Appleton-Century, 1929.

Tinker, Edward Larocque. *Creole City: Its Past and Its People*. New York: Longmans, Green, 1953.

ARCHITECTURE

Bruce, Curt. *Great Houses of New Orleans*. New York: Knopf, 1977.

Cable, Mary. *Lost New Orleans*. Boston: Houghton, Mifflin. 1980.

Gallier, James. *Autobiography of James Gallier, Architect*. Ed. Samuel Wilson. New York: DaCapo, 1973.

Huber, Leonard. *The Basilica on Jackson Square: The History of the St. Louis Cathedral and Its Predecessors 1727–1965*. New Orleans: St. Louis Cathedral, 1965.

Huber, Leonard. *The St. Louis Cemeteries of New Orleans.* New Orleans: St. Louis Cathedral, 1973.

Huber, Leonard Victor, and Guy F. Bernard. *To Glorious Immortality: the Rise and Fall of the Girod Street Cemetery, New Orleans First Protestant Cemetery, 1822–1957.* New Orleans: Alblen Books, 1961.

Huber, Leonard, and Samuel Wilson, Jr. *Baroness Pontalba's Buildings and the Remarkable Woman Who Built Them.* New Orleans: Friends of the Cabildo, n.d.

Huber, Leonard, and Samuel Wilson. *Cabildo on Jackson Square.* New Orleans: Friends of the Cabildo, 1970.

Kirk, Susan and Helen Smith. *The Architecture of St. Charles Avenue.* New Orleans: Pelican, 1977.

Latrobe, Benjamin. *Impressions Respecting New Orleans: Diary and Sketches, 1818–1820.* New York: Columbia Univ. Press, 1951.

Ledner, Albert C., ed. *A Guide to New Orleans Architecture.* New Orleans: American Institute of Architects, 1974.

New Orleans Architecture Series. New Orleans: Pelican Press.
   Wilson, Samuel, Jr., et al. *The Lower Garden District.* Vol. I. 1971.
   Christovich, Mary Louise, et al. *The American Sector.* Vol. II. 1972.
   Christovich, Mary Louise, et al. *Cemeteries.* Vol. III. 1974.
   Toledano, Roulhac, et al. *The Creole Faubourg.* Vol. IV. 1974.
   Christovich, Mary Louise. *Esplanade Ridge.* Vol. V. 1977.

Ricciuti, Italo William. *New Orleans and Its Environs: The Domestic Architecture, 1727–1870.* New York: Bonanza Books, 1938.

Samuel, Martha. *The Great Days of the Garden District and the Old City of Lafayette.* New Orleans: Louise S. McGehee School, 1961.

Scully, Arthur. *James Dakin, Architect: His Career in New York and the South.* Baton Rouge: Louisiana State Univ., 1973.

Wilson, Samuel, Jr. *A Guide to the Early Architecture of New Orleans.* New Orleans: Author, n.d.

Wilson, Samuel, Jr., *The Vieux Carre: New Orleans, Its Plan, Its Growth, Its Architecture.* New Orleans: Bureau of Governmental Research, 1968.

ART

Chancellor, John. *Audubon.* New York: Viking, 1978.

Ford, Alice. *John James Audubon.* Norman: Univ. of Oklahoma Press, 1964.

Ford, Alice. *The 1826 Journal of John James Audubon.* Norman: Univ. of Oklahoma Press, 1976.

Groves, W. E. *Louisiana Painters and Painting, 19th Century.* New Orleans: Pelican, 1971.

Mugnier, George F. *Louisiana Images 1880–1920.* Baton Rouge: Louisiana State Univ. Press, 1975.

Mugnier, George F. *New Orleans and Bayou Country: Photographs (1880–1910).* Barre, Mass.: Barre Publishers, 1972.

Ormond, S., and M. Irvine. *Louisiana's Art Nouveau: The Crafts of the Newcomb Style*. New Orleans: Pelican, 1976. These world famous crafts began with the women's liberation movement of the 1884 World Cotton Exposition.

MUSIC AND THEATER

Cable, George Washington. *The Dance in Place Congo*. New Orleans: Aurian, 1974.

Gottschalk, Louis Moreau. *Notes of a Pianist*. Ed. Jeanne Behrend. New York: Knopf, 1964.

Kendall, John S. *The Golden Age of the New Orleans Theater*. Baton Rouge: Louisiana State Univ. Press, 1952.

Kmen, Henry Arnold. *Music in New Orleans: The Formative Years, 1791–1841*. Baton Rouge: Louisiana State Univ. 1966.

Loggins, Vernon. *Where the World Ends: The Life of Louis Moreau Gottschalk*. Baton Rouge: Louisiana State Univ. Press, 1977.

Panzeri, Louis. *Louisiana Composers*. New Orleans: Dinstuhl, 1972.

Schafer, William J. *Brass Bands and New Orleans Jazz*. Baton Rouge: Louisiana State Univ. Press, 1977.

Smither, Nelle. *A History of the English Theatre in New Orleans*. New York: Benjamin Blom, 1944.

LITERATURE

Cable, George Washington. *Creoles and Cajuns: Stories of Old Louisiana*. Gloucester, Mass.: Peter Smith, 1965.

Cable, George Washington. *The Grandissimes*. New York: Charles Scribners, 1880.

Cable, George Washington. *Old Creole Days*. New York: Scribners, 1879.

Chopin, Kate. *The Complete Works of Kate Chopin*. 2 vols. Baton Rouge: Louisiana State Univ. Press, 1969.

Davis, M. E. M. *The Little Chevalier*. Boston: Houghton, Mifflin, 1903.

Holditch, W. Kenneth. *A Literary Tour of the French Quarter: New Orleans, Louisiana*. Urbana, Illinois: National Council of Teachers of English, 1974. The author is currently preparing for publication a more complete study of New Orleans in literature.

King, Grace. *Grace King of New Orleans: A Selection of Her Writings*. Ed. Robert Bush. Baton Rouge: Louisiana State Univ. Press, 1980.

King, Grace. *Memories of a Southern Woman of Letters*. New York: Macmillan, 1932.

Rouquette, Adrien Emmanuel. *Critical Dialogue Between Aboo and Caboo on a New Book, or A Grandissime Ascension*. New Orleans: Author, 1880. A defense of the Creoles against George Washington Cable's *Grandissimes*.

Rouquette, Adrien Emmanuel. *La Nouvelle Atala; ou, La Fille de L'esprit: Legende, Indienne par Chata-uma.* New Orleans: Author, 1879. A novel of the Choctaw Tribe.

Rouquette, Francois Dominique. *Fleurs d'Ameriques, Poesies Nouvelles.* New Orleans: Meridier, 1857.

Rubin, Louis D., Jr. *George W. Cable: The Life and Times of a Southern Heretic.* New York: Pegasus, 1969.

Saxon, Lyle. *Gumbo Ya-Ya: A Collection of Louisiana Folk Tales.* Boston: Houghton, 1945.

Tinker, Edward Larocque. *Lafcadio Hearn's American Days.* New York: Dodd, Mead, 1924.

Turner, Arlin. *George W. Cable, a Biography.* Durham, North Carolina: Duke Univ., 1956. Published in paperback by Louisiana State Univ. Press.

Vignes, Lois, ed. *Ladies of Louisiana.* New Orleans: Aurian Press, 1978. Short stories and essays by and about women in Louisiana during the 18th and 19th Centuries. Includes Hearn, Cable, Chopin, King, etc.

MARDI GRAS

Huber, Leonard. *Mardi Gras: A Pictorial History of Carnival in New Orleans.* New Orleans: Pelican, 1977.

Tallant, Robert. *Mardi Gras.* Garden City, N.Y.: Doubleday, 1948.

Young, Perry. *Mistick Krewe: Chronicles of Comus and His Kin, 1931.* New Orleans: Louisiana Heritage Press, 1969.

MEDICINE

Duffy, John. *Sword of Pestilence: The New Orleans Yellow Fever Epidemic of 1853.* Baton Rouge: Louisiana State Univ., 1966.

Wilds, John. *Crises, Clashes, and Cures: A Century of Medicine in New Orleans.* New Orleans Parish Medical Society, n.d.

RELIGION AND EDUCATION

Detiege, Sr. Audrey Marie. *Henriette Delille: Free Woman of Color.* New Orleans: Sisters of the Holy Family, 1976. History of the order with a biography of the foundress.

Dyer, John P. *Tulane: The Biography of a University, 1834–1965.* New York: Harper, 1966.

Huber, Leonard. *Our Lady of Guadalupe: The International Shrine of St. Jude. 150th Anniversary Edition 1826–1976.* Hackensack, N. J.: Custombook, 1976.

J. M. J. *The Ursulines in New Orleans and Our Lady of Prompt Succor: A Record of Two Centuries, 1827–1925.* New York: P. J. Kennedy, 1925.

Nolan, Charles E. *Bayou Carmel: The Sisters of Mount Carmel of Louisiana 1833–1903*. New Orleans: Archdiocese of New Orleans, 1977.

THE PEOPLE

Arthur, Stanley Clisby. *Old Families of Louisiana*. 1931; rpt. Baton Rouge: Claitor's, 1971.

Cable, George Washington. *The Creoles of Louisiana*. New York: Charles Scribner's Sons, 1910.

Copeland, Fayette. *Kendall of the Picayune: Being His Adventures in New Orleans, On the Texan Santa Fe Expedition, in the Mexican War, and in the Colonization of the Texas Frontier*. Norman: Univ. of Oklahoma Press, 1943.

Dufour, Charles L. *Women Who Cared: The 100 years of the Christian Woman's Exchange*. New Orleans: Christian Woman's Exchange, 1980.

Englehardt, George Washington. *The City of New Orleans*. New Orleans: Author, 1894. The Book of the Chamber of Commerce and Industry of Louisiana and Other Public Bodies of the "Crescent City."

Harmon, Nolan B. *The Famous Case of Myra Clark Gaines*. Baton Rouge: Louisiana State Univ. Press, 1964.

Hearn, Lafcadio. *"Gombo Zhebes": Little Dictionary of Creole Proverbs, Selected from Six Creole Dialects*. 1885; rpt. New Orleans: Aurian Society Publication, 1977.

Jewell, Edwin L., ed. *Jewell's Crescent City, Illustrated: the Commercial, Social, Political and General History of New Orleans, Including Biographical Sketches of its Distinguished Citizens, Together with a Map and General Strangers' Guide*. New Orleans: Author, 1873.

King, Grace Elizabeth. *Creole Families of New Orleans*. 1921; rpt. Baton Rouge: Claitor's, 1971.

King, Grace E. *New Orleans: The Place and the People*. New York: Macmillan, 1895.

Korn, Bertram Wallace. *The Early Jews of New Orleans*. Waltham, Mass.: American Jewish Historical Society, 1969.

Landry, Stuart O. *History of the Boston Club*. New Orleans: Pelican, 1928.

Lawson, David. *Paul Morphy: The Pride and Sorrow of Chess*. New York: McKay, 1977.

Miceli, Augusto P. *The Pickwick Club of New Orleans*.New Orleans: Pickwick Press, 1964.

Mount, May V. *Some Notables of New Orleans: Biographical and Descriptive Sketches of the Artists of New Orleans and Their Work. Illustrated with Extracts from the Works of Poets and Dramatists. Art in Music, Painting, Sculpture, Poetry, and the Drama*. New Orleans: Author, 1896.

Nau, John F. *The German People of New Orleans*. Lieden, Netherlands: E. J. Brill, 1958.

Ripley, Eliza. *Social Life in Old New Orleans: Being Recollections of My Girlhood*. New York: D. Appleton, 1912.

Saxon, Lyle. *Fabulous New Orleans*. New Orleans: Robert L. Crager, 1928.
Tallant, Robert. *The Romantic New Orleanians*. New York: E. P. Dutton, 1950.
Yujnovich, Milos M. *Yugoslavs in Louisiana*. New Orleans: Pelican, 1974.

LAGNIAPPE

Basso, Etolia S. *The World from Jackson Square*. New York: Farrar, Straus, 1948. An anthology of writings about New Orleans from the founding of the Colony up to the Forties.
Chase, John. *Frenchmen, Desire, Good Children and Other Streets of New Orleans*. New Orleans: Robert L. Crager, 1960.
Cocke, Edward. *Monumental New Orleans*. New Orleans: Hope, 1974.
Guilbeau, J. L. *The St. Charles Street Car of the New Orleans and Carrollton Railroad*. New Orleans: Author, 1975.
Hearn, Lafcadio. *Creole Cook Book*. 1885; rpt. New Orleans: Pelican, 1967.
Hennick, Louis, and Harper E. Charlton. *Street Railways of Louisiana*. New Orleans, La.: Pelican, 1978.
Hennick, Louis, and Harper E. Charlton. *The Streetcars of New Orleans*. New Orleans, La.: Pelican, 1975.
Huber, Leonard. *Lakeview Lore*. New Orleans: National Bank of Commerce, 1973.
Kane, Harnett T. *Gone are the Days*. New York: Bramhall House, 1960.
Kane, Harnett T. *Queen New Orleans, City by the River*. New York: Morrow, 1949.
Martinez, Raymond J. *Mysterious Marie Laveau: Voodoo Queen and Folk Tales along the Mississippi*. New Orleans: Hope, n.d.
Meyer, Robert. *Names Over New Orleans Public Schools*. New Orleans: Namesake Press, 1975.
Robinson, Lura. *It's an Old New Orleans Custom*. New York: Vanguard, 1948.
Rose, Al. *Storyville, New Orleans: Being an Authentic, Illustrated Account of the Notorious Red-Light District*. Tuscaloosa, Al.: Univ. of Alabama Press, 1974.
Searight, Sarah. *New Orleans*. New York: Stein & Day, 1973.
Somers, Dale A. *The Rise of Sports in New Orleans 1850–1900*. Baton Rouge: Louisiana State Univ. Press, 1972.
Tallant, Robert. *Voodoo in New Orleans*. New York: Macmillan, 1946.
Times Picayune. *The Picayune Creole Cook Book*. "To assist the good housewives of the present day and to preserve to future generations the many excellent and matchless recipes of the New Orleans Cuisine by gathering up from the old Creole cooks and the old housekeepers the best of Creole Cookery, with all its delightful combinations and possibilities, is the object of this book." New Orleans: Times-Picayune Publishing Company, 1901.
U.S. Government. *Report of the Select Committee on the New Orleans Riots*. 1867; rpt. Freeport, N.Y.: Books for Libraries Press, 1971.

Notes on Contributors

JUDITH HOPKINS BONNER, a graduate of Newcomb College, Tulane University, wrote her thesis on George David Coulon and his family. Recently, she has read papers at the South-Central Renaissance Conference and the South-Central Conference on Christianity and Literature.

THOMAS BONNER, JR. teaches at Xavier University of Louisiana, where he is professor and chairman of English. His most recent publication is *William Faulkner: The William B. Wisdom Collection*. His articles on Kate Chopin have appeared in *Bulletin of Bibliography* and *The Markham Review*, among others.

EUGENE D. CIZEK is a practicing architect and a professor at Tulane University. He has published extensively in his field, especially as related to the importance of history for providing guidelines for urban change and growth and the subsequent impact on the urban resident. He is active in the areas of preservation and restoration in the city of New Orleans.

KAYE DEMETZ teaches speech and drama at Mercy College in the New York area and performs and choreographs for off-off-Broadway productions in New York City.

ALFRED J. GUILLUAME, JR. is dean of arts and sciences at Xavier University of Louisiana and assistant professor of French. He has published in *New Laurel Review, French Review* and *The College Language Association Journal*.

W. KENNETH HOLDITCH, a native of Mississippi, is professor of English at the University of New Orleans. He conducts literary tours of New Orleans and is currently at work on a study of authors and works associated with the city.

PEGGY MCDOWELL is an associate professor of art at the University of New Orleans. She co-authored *New Orleans Architecture III The Cemeteries* and has recently completed a manuscript on American Monuments and Memorials for future publication.

187

GEORGE REINECKE, is a professor of English at the University of New Orleans. Mainly of French descent, he grew up in the Esplanade section of New Orleans and spoke French before English. He is a third generation member of Dr. Mercier's Athenee Louisianais. He has recently edited Henry Castellanos' *New Orleans As It Was* for the LSU Press.

COLEEN COLE SALLEY teaches library science at the University of New Orleans, where she specializes in children's literature, and has traveled extensively teaching courses in the field. She recently received the Louisiana State University system Distinguished Faculty award.